NEWSPAPERS & PR

A MEDIA LIFE

NIGEL HEATH

Copyright © Nigel Heath 2023

This book is sold subject to the condition that it shall not, by way of trade or otherwise, be lent, resold, hired out, or otherwise circulated without the publisher's prior consent in any form of binding or cover other than that in which it is published and without a similar condition including this condition being imposed on the subsequent publisher.
The moral right of Nigel Heath has been asserted.

ISBN: 9798853898776

ACKNOWLEDGEMENTS

Firstly, a big thank you to, BBC Radio Bristol Presenter, Steve Yabsley, whose enthusiasm for a student visit he made to the city's busy Bristol Evening Post news room in pre-internet days, and a later interview on his Sunday afternoon programme inspired me to write this book.

My grateful thanks also to my journalist colleague, friend, walking companion and poet, Peter Gibbs, who was Assistant Editor, of the Post's rival sister paper, the Western Daily Press, during my 17 reporting years with, the then Bristol United Press.

Peter, who later joined me for some years after I had launched my news media PR enterprise, Media-Consult, was responsible for the editing and production of this book.

CONTENTS

FOREWORD..5

JOINING THE SOUTH AVON MERCURY...............................7

IN THE WIDER WORLD..29

JOINING THE BRISTOL EVENING POST............................42

THE SWISS AIR DISASTER...59

PRESS TRIPS..67

BECOMING A SHIPPING CORRESPONDENT......................77

MY PR YEARS..105

NEW BEGINNINGS & THE BIG SLEEP YEARS...................124

TREASURE ISLAND...135

WORKING WITH AMTRAK..141

ROCCO FORTE HOTELS & TRANSUN..............................147

OUR OTHER HOTEL YEARS..154

CRIBBS CAUSEWAY..156

OFFICE LIFE..159

EPILOGUE...166

STOP PRESS..168

FOREWORD

I have always endeavoured during all my reporting and PR years, to follow up ASAP, or in most cases, right there and then, when a small voice in my head has suggested I should take some form of action.

So it was, that aged 18, I was walking down, Clevedon's Hill Road, a busy shopping centre in those far off days, when I suddenly spotted a green Victorian lamp post, standing in the pavement.

The strange thing was, that although I had lived in Clevedon, since I was aged six, and had walked down that road many thousands of times, I had never spotted that post before.

"Why don't you write a letter to the Editor of the South Avon Mercury, explaining this astonishing fact and wondering if any other readers were in my position?" my little voice suggested.

So, I went home, right there and then, and did exactly what my 'voice,' had suggested.

The following Saturday, I wandered into Seeley's, the popular Hill Road newsagents and stationery shop, back in those days, and surreptitiously made my way to the back of the shop, where I picked up a copy of the paper and began thumbing through the pages.

Imagine my surprise and the absolute thrill I got when I saw my letter there, for all to read, and I knew right there and then, that becoming a journalist was the only career for me!

As fate and good fortune would have it, the Mercury's current junior reporter had just gained his required NCTJ proficiency certificate and would be leaving, so a vacancy was being created.

Luckily for me, the entry requirement was just one A level, which I had just scraped past in History, and even luckier the Editor, Victor Smith, agreed to take me on for a three-month trial, and the rest as they say, is also history!

JOINING THE SOUTH AVON MERCURY

I started as a probationary junior reporter on the South Avon Mercury on a Monday morning in June, 1966, aged 19.

The bus journey from my home in the North Somerset village of Congresbury, was somehow reminiscent of that other important Monday morning, years earlier, when I travelled with my school friend, Alan Lane, from Hill Road, nearby in Clevedon, to St Andrew's Junior School for the first time.

It was scary then and it was equally scary now because new beginnings often are.

I had completely lost touch with my childhood friend, Alan, and had not given him a thought for years, yet now I was about to discover that his kindly father, John. was in fact the General Manager of the South Avon Mercury and Printing Company.

I entered the Mercury's front office in leafy Linden Road and stood at the wooden front counter, from which I would later take down many a story of town life.

"I'm the new reporter," I told the receptionist, the sprightly Mrs Kite, whose son, Max, I had also known at Junior School.

"Well, you had better go on up then," she said indicating a door leading to an entrance hall and stairs.

Up I went and turned left, as instructed, and into a large and airy room, where two people, whom I quickly came to know as, Richard and Liz, were busy with a book binding operation.

I introduced myself again and they showed me through into the reporters' room and left me, while they got on with their work.

I was clearly the first to arrive, so I just stood there and looked around me, not knowing quite what else to do.

It was a strange and uncomfortable moment, somehow poised on the brink of a completely new life.

The room was large and had two big windows, one offering a fine view of the busy traffic island and the other, looking out over the town's Six Ways bus terminus, was fronted by a crude trestle table dominated by a large glass ashtray, a couple of newspapers, and a pile of typewritten sheets held together with paperclips.

Along the wall to my left, was a sloping counter with several newspapers open on it.

The body of the room had six other desks, five of which had large and now silent typewriters of various makes and ages.

I suddenly became aware of heavy uneven footsteps and a puffing and a panting as, Bert Newton, a veteran sub-editor of the old Bristol Evening World, having climbed the office stairs, came limping into the room and into my life.

He collapsed into his chair in front of the glass ashtray and gave me an inquiring look.

"I'm Nigel the new reporter," I said again, not waiting for the obvious question.

Bert nodded and went on getting his breath back. Next to enter was Nick Bull, a young reporter, who had recently passed his proficiency test and whose place I would be taking.

He was the son of the Hill Road pet shop proprietor and again I already knew him from my childhood days, when I lived with my mum and dad and siblings, Bernadette, and Roger, in a maisonette in Kings Road, just below Dial Hill.

We had moved down from Bristol when I was aged six, initially into a former converted bathhouse in the grounds of the now long-demolished Edgarley Hotel, opposite the Roman Catholic Church, where I was to spend many long and tedious childhood hours.

While the old bathhouse had fabulous views out over the town's Victorian pier and across to the Welsh coast, it was extremely damp, so a few years later we had moved along Wellington Terrace, with its row of beautiful Victorian villas, and up to Kings Road.

Sadly, my father. John, collapsed and died of a cerebral haemorrhage when I was just 14 and a couple of years later, we moved over to Congresbury to live rent-free in Stonewell Farm, owned by a cousin.

Nick was followed into the reporters' room by, Diana Cambridge, another youngster, who, I quickly discovered, was good at writing features and who lived with her parents in nearby Elton Road.

A few moments later, the editorial team was completed with the arrival of Mervyn Davies, the slightly rotund and much-loved chief reporter, who was known for miles around.

Mervyn also lived in Congresbury and had spent many years as a solicitor's clerk in Bristol, while devoting virtually all his free time to writing sports reports for the Mercury and its arch rival, the Weston Mercury.

He was a prolific and tireless writer, who spent most of his Saturdays, and virtually all his Sundays, churning out endless columns on local cricket, snooker, darts, skittles, and cribbage - all his favourite past times - and for which he was paid linage or so many pence per line.

Mervyn eventually decided to acknowledge where his true interests lay and, after, I think, a time working as a reporter for the Weston Mercury, he accepted an invitation from Victor Smith to become Chief Reporter of the South Avon Mercury.

I have never met a more generous and kind-hearted man than Mervyn, who would always go out of his way to do anyone a favour.

He picked me up for work from Stonewell Farm every morning and was forever stopping to give lifts to his seemingly endless stream of friends and acquaintances.

This handy arrangement continued until I inherited Nick's blue and white moped, when he went off to join his first daily newspaper, The Herald Express in Torquay.

Mervyn was extremely proud of being Welsh and of his birthplace, the tiny village of Mountain Ash, in South Wales, and of having served in Burma during World War Two.

After the initial introductions were made, I was given a desk with an old sit-up-and- beg typewriter, complete with ink ribbon and worn-out keys, and asked to write a piece about the first summer visit of the paddle steamer, Bristol Queen, to Clevedon Pier at the weekend.

So, the moment I had been waiting for, had come at last.

Since moving to the area, P&A Campbell's Bristol Queen and her sister paddler, Cardiff Queen, had been familiar sights sailing in and out of my life every summer and I had many happy memories of trips across to Penarth and down channel to Ilfracombe and occasionally on to land on Lundy Island.

So, with bated breath and my fingers fumbling for those keys I wrote: "If you should have been walking along Clevedon's promenade last Sunday afternoon, you might well have seen the paddle steamer, Bristol Queen, making her first call of the season at the town's Victorian pier."

I went on to tell readers that the sailing had been well supported and gave some details of future sailings, as mentioned in the press release I had been handed.

Doing as I was instructed, I typed the first three paragraphs on separate pieces of copy paper and then followed on with three or four more 'pars' per sheet until the story was finished,

Then I secured my first-ever 'copy' together with a paper clip and took it over and with much apprehension, placed it on the pile for Bert to sub.

I guess I had better stop here and explain that it was a sub-editor's job to read a reporter's copy, check it for spelling and punctuation, shorten it if necessary and then write a headline with setting instructions for the printers, who in our case were on the floor below.

Bert, who chain-smoked a particularly pungent brand of French cigarettes, which I would later collect for him from the tobacconist opposite, eventually took up my piece, looked at it for a moment and then called me over.

"Now look," he said in a kindly almost fatherly voice: "If you had been the first to come on the scene of a house on fire and were later telling friends about it, would you say: I was walking down the street this morning and spotted a house on fire?

"No, you would say: I've just seen a house on fire. So, remember you must always put the most important fact first, which in this case is that the paddle steamer Bristol Queen made her first visit to Clevedon Pier on Sunday."

He gave me back my copy and I went and sat down and wrote it all over again.

"Always try to answer the questions, who, what, where, when and why in the first few paragraphs, I was told.

My first task, on subsequent Monday mornings, was to call up all the local Funeral Directors on our patch, covering the towns of Clevedon, Nailsea, Portishead and the villages of Yatton and Congresbury, to see who had died and Bert Price from my own village was one of my favourites.

"Hello Nigel," he would say in his deep, rich voice: "I'm the lonely and out of work undertaker, cos I ain't got nobody!"
The undertakers were generally a cheerful and friendly bunch, which, I suppose, goes with the territory.

Being faced with one's own mortality on a daily basis would be no good for someone who was depressive by nature, I guess.

When Bert, or any of his colleagues did have a "customer", they would give me the name and telephone number of the nearest relative and I would call them to ask if they would like an obituary written.

Telephoning people, who were deeply distressed, or in shock, if there had been a sudden death in the family, was quite daunting for a 19-year-old, but it quickly taught me how to act with gentle sympathy, while remaining somehow detached.

I was not aware of it at the time, but this was excellent training for dealing with some of the harrowing experiences, which were to follow later in my career.

At the end of the interview, I would ask if the family wanted a list of mourners taken at the church door, and also a list of the floral tributes, and if the answer to both questions was "yes," then that meant I was in for a particularly unpleasant time.

If the deceased was a prominent local citizen, then Nick or Diana would turn out to help me take the names, but mostly I was left to face this, often daunting, challenge alone.

I will never, ever forget that first cloudy summer morning when I arrived at Clevedon's St Andrew's Parish Church, notebook in hand.

To start with all appeared to be going rather well - I placed myself, as instructed, in such a position that no one could enter the church without their name being taken.

But I was not prepared for the added complication of the people, who were also representing somebody else!

My writing has never been very good and even today friends often just guess that Christmas cards are from me, so I was taking a little time to write the mourners' names, so that I could actually read them later.

A small and orderly queue had started forming in front of me, but no one was champing at the bit because they were obviously used to this procedure.

I tried to stay calm and went on writing, although I could feel the first little sensation of panic beginning to stir in my stomach.

Mrs Jean Forbes-Brown, also representing the ladies sewing circle and the Women's Bright Hour, was quickly followed by Major Dobbs, also representing Colonel J Harris and Mrs Harris.

"Excuse-me, Major, could I have your Christian name," I asked, but it was no good because he had already brushed past me and entered the church, by which time I had forgotten the names of those he was also representing.

Then to my horror, I saw that the cortege with the flower-covered coffin had already assembled at the bottom of the church path and was about to begin its procession.

I quickly took down a few more names. "I am the way, the truth and the light.", I heard the vicar begin to chant.

The remaining mourners had also heard it and started looking anxiously over their shoulders and I knew then that all was now lost.

I closed my notebook and darted out of the church porch in the face of the advancing column and retreated to relative safety among the gravestones.

It began to rain as I made my way miserably to the nearby open grave and started trying to read the names on the floral wreaths.

Hang on a minute - was I supposed to just take down the names or had I been told to write out the sympathy messages as well? I simply could not remember.

"God is My Shepherd, I shall not want," the congregation began to sing out with gusto from within those hallowed walls.

I looked frantically around me. There were over 30 wreaths scattered about. It must surely be only the names, I concluded, crouching down and beginning to read the little white cards.

My hands were now wet from handling the flowers and the ink in my notebook was starting to run.

Was that an 'e' or was it an 'a' I asked myself trying to decipher some of the, often scrawled, handwriting?

This miserable task was eventually completed and I walked slowly and dejectedly back to the office feeling a complete failure and knowing full well that the telephone would probably start ringing the following week when outraged mourners saw that they had been left off the wretched list.

The St Andrew's Church is just along the road from Clevedon's Salthouse Fields and Salthouse Hotel and, as I walked past on that damp morning, I was suddenly reminded of a similar morning, when as a 14-year-old I had gone to the hotel on my bike to do some gardening.

But it had been raining and digging the rose garden border, the task I had been given by the landlord, was impossible to carry out because the soil was too heavy.

I told him so, and rode dejectedly away.

So, no cash was going to be earned and I was feeling down in the dumps, when suddenly a watery sun popped out from behind a cloud and my spirits lifted because tomorrow was another day.

The office phone rang for me just before I was about to go home and to my surprise it was the deceased's wife.

"I'm sorry to trouble you," she said. Oh! hell, she was calling to complain about the mess up in the porch, I thought.

"I was very pleased that you took the time and trouble to come and take the names at the church, but my sister doesn't want them or the floral tributes in the paper. She thinks it's being pretentious."

So I had been saved at the eleventh hour by another of those extraordinary pieces of good fortune, which tend to come my way.

Luckily, the Mercury decided to drop publishing floral tributes, unless the undertakers supplied a typewritten list.

Another undertaking story I shall never forget arrived by way of a letter of complaint to the editor.

It was from an outraged lady in South Wales, who had been over to say farewell to her dead brother and had found, to her horror, that the undertaker's Chapel of Rest was 'no better than a garden shed.'

By now I was on Christian name terms with all the undertakers, so I had no hesitation in riding over to Nailsea on my newly-inherited moped and showing this letter to the alleged offender.

"My Chapel of Rest like a garden shed. Ah!," he said through gritted teeth. "Well, sonny, you had better come and see it for yourself."

I dutifully followed him around to the back of his premises and in through a door.

It was very cold in this chapel-like room and there on a trestle table was an open coffin.

Its occupant was an elderly grey-haired lady, whose tranquil face was instantly etched on my memory forever.

I pretended I had not noticed her, although the undertaker knew that I had.

I made a great show of looking all around and then we left and I returned thoughtfully to the office, having had my first encounter with a dead body.

I have to say with complete honesty that the Chapel of Rest was simply and tastefully decorated and fitted out as far as my young and inexperienced eyes could see and I could not understand what this lady was making all the fuss about.

So her letter was consigned to the office spike, an evil looking, but deadly efficient implement, consisting of a nine-inch sharpened length of metal facing upwards from a block of wood.

Collecting endless lists of names, like those at church doors was, I quickly discovered, the bread and butter for local newspapers, because people liked seeing their names in print, so I did so at every available opportunity that first Mercury summer.

I went along to village fetes and took down the names of all the stall holders, attended horse shows and gymkhanas and made even more lists of event winners and runners-up and drove on my moped to flower shows in towns and villages all over North Somerset.

Here I took even more copious notes, recording the winners and runners-up in hundreds and hundreds of different classes, but while those lists were extremely tedious, they invariably gave me the introduction to that particular story.

Green-fingered Mr Bert Brooks swept the board in the dahlia classes at such–and- such a flower show, or Miss Milly Long jumped to victory in the open section of X,Y or Z gymkhana, I learnt to write.

Virtually all these events, including numerous carnivals, were held on Saturdays, so what with all the town, district and parish council meetings held on weekday evenings, I nearly always worked six or even seven-day weeks during the summer months.

Part of every Sunday had to be spent writing up all the Saturday jobs, because Bert always needed them to start filling the early pages on Monday mornings.

But riding out on my trusty moped on glorious summer evenings to attend yet another long and dreary parish council meeting, having worked all day in the office, did take some dedication, especially as I would then have to go home and sit up into the early hours writing the copy.

Mastering the technique of writing a story in the format required by Bert did not come at all easy to me during that first summer.

It would often be gone 2am when I crawled into bed, reasonably confident that I had written all the pieces about vandalism at the local bus shelter, litter on the village green and various drainage and other problems, in such a way that Bert would not have to cover them with red ink to lick them into shape.

But at some magical point, and I can't remember quite when, the penny did eventually drop, so much so that it was to later lead to the first and only bit of praise I was ever to receive during my years of training.

I knew I was not of the calibre of Nick or Diana, who were both bright youngsters, but I struggled on and managed to pass the first hurdle of getting myself indentured as a trainee reporter after the initial three-month trial.

I think this was mainly because I worked hard and did my best and, although I was not particularly promising, it would probably have been too much hassle to go through the appointment process all over again.

Editor Victor Smith told me as much by explaining in a roundabout way that the promising lad that he had really wanted had turned him down at the last minute.

Although attending all those evening meetings was a chore, I had already been deeply infected by the almost indescribable thrill of finding a really good story, which I could be the first to reveal to an unsuspecting world.

Most of these evenings were dull affairs, but then I was faced with the challenge of making the best of what ever there was, and trying to come up with an interesting angle.

As time marched on, I got faster and faster at producing copy and eventually mastered the technique of writing one story while keeping an ear open on the proceedings and making quick notes on the subject under discussion.

Most news stories are no more than twelve or fifteen pars long, so one did not need copious notes, because it was simply a question of getting down all the bullet points and then stringing them together in order of importance, I eventually discovered.

But that was all to be a little into the future for this callow 19-year-old, still struggling to get to grips with all that it meant to be a junior reporter in that far away summer of 1966.

To start with, being a reporter, even a very junior one, made me feel a someone instead of being a hopeless no one, who had almost always been bottom of the class and a big disappointment to his long-suffering father.

The trouble was that, having failed my 11-Plus examination and seen most of my friends disappear off to Nailsea Grammar School, I went to Clevedon Secondary Modern school, which had a totally inflexible examination system in the early Sixties.

At the end of every term there were ten exam subjects, each carrying 100 marks, and as three of them were Maths related and two others covered Science and Technical Drawing, my chances of not ending up close to the bottom, if not bottom of the class, were minimal.

But now I had been unwittingly elevated into being a very minor personality in the local community, who possessed the power to turn people's triumphs, grievances, and tragedies into the written word and on a page for all the world to see.

Doors were suddenly and magically swinging open in all directions as I was invited to a host of local functions and began getting to know all the people, who made the community tick, from the town's fire chief and council chairman, through to the president of the chamber of trade, and the leading lights in the town's charity organisations.

Despite all the hard work, long hours, and my early tortuous struggles with copy writing late into the night, it never ever entered my head that I should want to give up and try something else.

As you will have already noticed, a junior reporter on a weekly paper in those now far-off days literally learned the job from the bottom up and although the custom of taking names at church doors and making list of stall holders died out years ago, I don't believe there could have been a better way for me to start out on a career in journalism.

Besides those endless lists, Diana and I were sent out into the town to write advertising features on all the events, which mark the changing of the seasons.

My first introduction to this cyclical merry-go-round was the September Back to School promotion, quickly followed by the Autumn Sales, Christmas, Easter, and Spring Sales and so on around the calendar.

We worked on the lists of advertisers supplied by Hugh Drummond, the Mercury's enthusiastic young advertising manager, who was later succeeded by the always lively, Paddy Coles.

Paddy, who was highly theatrical, would often come back to the office, sit down at his desk, and tell us in great and humorous detail how he had fared during the day, regaling us with tales and mimicking the voices of characters involved.

Trying to think up something original or interesting to say about an Autumn Sale in The Triangle, Hill Road and Alexandra Road shopping centres often taxed me to the limit, but it did mean I spent huge chunks of time out of the office talking to people and honing my interview skills and there was always the prospect that I would actually find a good story.

"My grandma's celebrated her hundredth birthday, but we think her letter from the Queen must have got lost in the post," one young woman florist told me.

Any proud family, with a soon-to-be centenarian – a rarity it seemed in those days - wrote in or called in and told us well in advance, but this one appeared to have sneaked under our radar.

Another of my duties, which I really enjoyed, was writing the weekly column looking back on the daily life of the town, as reported in the then broadsheet Clevedon Mercury over the past 100 hundred years,

This, amazing archive existed in a row of red leather or cloth-bound books, all lined up under a sloping panel, on top of which I heaved out and rested them.

My task was to copy out short pieces from the editions 100 years, 75 years, 50 years and 25 years ago.

Naturally, on my first foray into the past, I turned the pages as far back as I could possibly go to read in graphic detail, all about the last public hanging of some poor individual in the nearby village of Kenn, which I seem to recall was for the heinous crime of stealing a sheep, but I might be wrong.

Annoyingly this story was, I think about 125 years ago, at and therefore beyond my remit,

However, what I did discover, was that the unknown and unsung scribes of 1865 were more heavily into making lists than I was, because there were long columns noting the arrival of new residents to houses in the town and the departure of others.

I can just imagine this sort of intelligence being avidly seized upon by the class-conscious Victorian folk, who inhabited the large and imposing mansions.

Whenever I had a quiet half hour, I would heave one of the heavy volumes up onto the reading desk, open it up to the current month and perch beside it on a high stool with my rickety typewriter in front of me and begin copying out any news item, which attracted my attention.

The arrivals of the paddle steamer, Ravenswood, at Clevedon Pier, a century before I was to write my first ever story about The Bristol Queen, were always reported as were the Petty Sessions at which miscreants were fined for poaching or being drunk, among many other crimes.

Once it became apparent that I was beginning to pick up the fundamentals of the job, I was allowed to start making the crucially-important morning calls to the Police, Fire and Ambulance Services, who were the real sources of the best hot news stories.

It was inevitable that our daily rivals, the Bristol Evening Post and Western Daily Press, would always be first with the hot news and that meant that we had to look for the follow-up angles.

Just occasionally our follow-ups would produce a better story than the original one, and then it was always gratifying to see the dailies turn around and follow up on us.

Here I must say that back in those days, being able to enjoy a relaxed working relationship with members of the emergency services was a real bonus, although, of course, we never appreciated it at the time.

That relationship was mostly based on mutual respect and trust and worked well for many years to come.

Today, all press enquiries have to be channelled through a single Force Communications Office and therefore are inevitably tightly controlled.

Not so long ago I gave a hot tip to a local reporter, but when noting appeared for a couple of days, I called him back to be told he was still waiting for a reply to his inquiry!

But our best chance of an "exclusive" story came from the off-diary happenings, which we might stumble across or were told about by our contacts.

These were a strange mix of people, who were naturally inquisitive and knew what was going on in the town, possessing an overwhelming desire to share their knowledge with us, in confidence, of course.

We all had our precious contacts books packed full of the telephone numbers of our special friends, for want of a better description, plus parish, town, and district councillors and all the other local notables, personalities and publicity-conscious characters, who inhabited our community.

Most lunch times, Mervyn and I, and sometimes Diana, would walk past the Clevedon Community Centre and down the hill to The Oak Room Café for lunch, while Bert would follow in his old red Fiat.

The oak-panelled dining room was on the first floor of the Curzon Cinema, where I had spent literally hundreds of hours watching Westerns and crime movies, while growing up in the town.

Every Saturday, my sister, Bernie, brother Roger and I would troop down the Zig-Zag path to Hill Road and then on down to the cinema for the special kids show and then often back again in the afternoon for the normal performance.

The Oak Room Cafe was presided over by the ever-expansive and extremely quick witted, Tommy Wilkinson.

He was also proprietor of Clevedon Catererers catering company and President of the Clevedon Pirates charity organisation, whose Latin motto loosely translated meant that members, mostly fellow traders. and business people, had a fun time, while raising cash for charity.

I had only been at the Mercury about a week, when I had my first encounter with the Pirates, who had invited the paper to cover their charity fund-raising narrow boat cruise from the Bristol city docks along the River Avon to Saltford.

I had no transport of my own at that time, so local grocer, Laundon Gray, kindly picked me up and dropped me off at home again afterwards.

It was my first-ever evening assignment and as we cruised along on that balmy summer evening, drinking beer and tucking into another of Clevedon Caterers' delicious spreads, I thought that life was, definitely looking up.

Tommy's quick wits were well matched by those of our veteran sub-editor, Bert, and the two kept up sometimes-insulting banter, which would often surprise and perplex café diners, who were not regulars and therefore not accustomed to this impromptu lunchtime entertainment.

"This is excellent soup, Tom," Bert said on one occasion, his spoon poised for another taste.

"How do you make it?" he asked "We don't make it," came the quick-fire response. "It accumulates."

On another occasion, Tommy strode down the room and presented the menu with a flourish and a slight bow, to a regular lady diner, who was always up for the crack, but was known to have an extremely delicate appetite.

"And what would madam like to leave today?" he asked beaming. We all roared with laughter and so did she.

By now I had also started attending the magistrates court at Long Ashton, at first in company with Mervyn, and then later, on my own, and this is where my recently-acquired copy of Essential Law for Journalists came very much into its own.

The extremely hard and uncomfortable wooden bench reserved for the Press was nearly always occupied by a senior reporter from the Evening Post.

If I had a query or had missed an important quote, then they were normally extremely helpful, unless, of course, they were racing to catch a deadline, in which case I usually knew better than to ask.

The court sat on Fridays and proceedings started at 10am and normally dragged on until around 1pm, by which time I had usually taken down and written up in long hand at least half a dozen stories.

My bag for the day mostly consisted of motorists, fined for speeding, or driving without due care and attention, through to minor shop-lifting offences and householders, who were being fined for failing to pay their television licences.

On a good day, there could be the local roughnecks in court for being drunk and disorderly or for a breach of the peace, following a punch-up, or occasionally, a good old-fashion case of fish poaching, which usually made a more interesting story.

I gradually came to know the court staff, including the magistrates' clerk and the black-gowned ushers, often retired policemen, and, of course, the defending and prosecuting solicitors, who were sometimes extremely colourful characters.

The proceedings were not without their share of drama, because the magistrates had the power to send a defendant to prison for up to six months and so I and the rest of the court waited and wondered while the members of the bench retired to consider whether to hand out a custodial sentence.

On these occasions it was often the case that one of the court's "regular" customers was up yet again for another petty theft and his long-suffering solicitor had made a last-ditch plea for him to be allowed to keep his liberty.

There were also the lighter moments, like the time it was suddenly noticed by sheer coincidence that all the participants in a particular case were named after our feathered friends including Bird, Crow, and Partridge!

One chairman of the bench, a magistrate of many years standing, once delighted in telling me the story of the time an old lag was up before him for urinating against the wall of the Clevedon Conservative Club.

His solicitor, a veteran of many appearances before the Long Ashton bench, explained that his client had taken a few drinks in The Drum and Monkey at Kenn and was on his way home, when nature had suddenly taken over and his bladder had not allowed him to wait a moment longer before relieving himself in front of the club.

"Ah" said this particular magistrate, keen to clarify the facts, "I thought that pub out at Kenn was called The Rose and Crown."

Instantly the solicitor responded with: "I bow to your worship's superior knowledge of pubs and drinking!"

While Long Ashton Magistrates' Court could always be relied upon to fill a good few of the Mercury's column inches, so could the local churches and their clergy, who were often a rich source of stories from church roof and tower repair appeals, through to their much fan fared arrivals and departures.

The more go-ahead, young and dynamic the vicar, then the bigger and more vibrant their congregations, or so it seemed to me, and there was nothing like a good church controversy to get everyone going and provide dozens of column inches.

Issues like the banning of plastic flowers from graves or any move to modernise or change any part of the fabric of a centuries old church, could virtually be guaranteed to stir up a hornets' nest among the die-hard traditionalists.

When the tower bells in the town's Christ Church eventually became unstable and too dangerous to ring, the vicar at the time proposed replacing them with electronic ones.

This was, of course, a red rag to the proverbial bull for many of the older worshippers, who kicked up such a fuss that the Bishop of Bath and Wells ordered the setting up of a Consistory or special Church Court.

It was the first and last time that I was ever to come across this procedure, which finally resulted in a judgement supporting the vicar, who was thus saved from having to spend a huge sum on tower repairs.
I quite soon discovered that fact could be stranger than fiction, like the time we had a call from an outraged Clevedon allotment holder, who had become the latest victim of the Phantom Tattie Snatcher.

This allotments raider with a strange sense of humour would dig up a helping of spuds in the dead of night and return later to leave a parcel of potato peelings as his or her calling card.

IN THE WIDER WORLD

In the wider world, the Queen had opened the first Severn Bridge, in September, 1966, a story which Nicky and Diana both covered before they left, and the famous Aust Ferry, on which I had travelled to Wales on several wet and windy occasions, had soon after been consigned to the pages of history.

By now the giant construction scar of the M5, a motorway in the making, was also steadily and relentlessly driving its way across the quiet North Somerset landscape.

Its attendant army of massive earth-carrying trucks, moved like giant ants in an endless line up and down the route, now forging its way across the landscape.

In what seemed an amazing feat of engineering at the time, the motorway builders blasted their way right through the hill separating the Gordano Valley from the village of Tickenham, and used the tens of thousands of tonnes of limestone to lay a path down across the flat and often boggy moor land between Clevedon and Yatton and beyond.

Part of my fondly-remembered childhood walk to the Iron Age fort at Cadbury Camp was sadly taken away forever to be replaced by a lofty foot and bridleway bridge upon which the occasional horse rider can be seen trotting high above the speeding traffic.

The building of the motorway across farmland naturally resulted in an often rich and continuous crop of stories from those affected, including some who feared that the road running down from Tickenham Hill would act as a giant storm water drain, so leading to large scale flooding.

Although this worry seemed a logical one at the time, it proved groundless.

There were some inevitable casualties, however, and one of these was the lovely old National Trust property, Clevedon Court, the home of the Elton family, then the owners of the Mercury.

The centuries-old building can now never escape from the noise of the traffic except, perhaps, late at night and very early in the morning.

If I ever lived with that dull and almost never-ending roar, I think I would try to imagine it was the sound of surf breaking on some distant sunlit shore.

When Diana passed her exams and left the Mercury to join her first evening paper and was not immediately replaced, I had to write up all the wedding reports from the forms, which we dished out to all the local photographers, and they in turn gave to the couples.

It was normally the bride's proud mother who filled in this questionnaire and the photographer then returned it to us with a picture of the happy couple, which we later published.

I often had to plough through half a dozen of these highly-detailed forms on a Monday morning, becoming bogged down in describing the bride's dress, the bridesmaids' dresses, what the couple's mothers wore, who gave the bride away, a description of the bride's bouquet and of those carried by the attendants, and so on and so on.

I had to be sure I got it all right because, if I made a single mistake, I could be sure that retribution would quickly follow with telephoned calls from outraged mums or mothers-in-law.

But even weddings could be made a little interesting if the bride and her dad arrived in a vintage car, pony and trap, or even a helicopter.

And then there was that particular Monday morning when I found myself staring at the picture of a bully, who had made my life such a misery when I first went to Clevedon Secondary School.

It was not Mercury policy in those days to give reporters by-lines so I had to wait until I joined the Bristol Evening Post to experience that initial thrill.

Writing my first lead story for my paper was a prize, which seemed to go on eluding me, as I plodded on with the never-ending round of weddings, funerals, advertising features, charity events, council meeting reports and local thefts.

Then one very wet Tuesday morning, it suddenly and magically happened.

I was on my way back from a funeral at St Andrew's Parish Church and was passing the Salthouse Fields when I noted the familiar sight of Joe Heal's travelling funfair.

Right from early childhood, the Bank Holiday arrival of the fair with its dodgems, gallopers, stalls, side shows and penny-in-the slot machines was a time of great excitement for us kids, but on this particular weekend, the weather had been absolutely atrocious, so it would have been no fun at all.

I stopped and went over to find a virtual sea of mud and, squelching towards me in a plastered pair of Wellingtons, came a very miserable Joe Heal.

We got a picture of Joe standing in the mud and I wrote the story, which Bert subbed and put up the Page One lead headline, "It Was Not Much Fun at the Fair on a Wet Weekend."

On another occasion towards the end of my time in Clevedon, I went off in the grey Mercury Minivan to cover the Queen's visit to the University of Bristol veterinary research station in Langford.

I was driving along the road between the villages of Yatton and my home in Congresbury, when I spotted a group of youngsters carrying Union Jacks.

I stopped and they told me they were off to see the Queen and, as it would be a round trip of at least six miles, it would make a nice little line for my piece whatever else came along.

Always keep your eyes wide open for possible story opportunities, we trainee reporters were told during the first week of our six-week block release course at Cardiff College.

Our tutor, a sub-editor from the large circulation, Birmingham Evening Mail, then sent us out to make a list of all the potential stories we could find within a mile radius of the college.

I decided to start right there on the campus and quickly discovered that students on a catering course in the next block had just won some award.

The Head of Catering got quite excited about the prospect of getting some publicity, until he was told by our tutor that this was simply meant to be a paper exercise and that I had taken it all a bit too far. Well at least I had got a real story, I thought.

We were also despatched to the Cardiff Crown Court to practise our shorthand note taking and to the theatre and cinema to write reviews and given tuition on local government and the laws of libel and slander.

'If in doubt, then leave it out,' was the golden rule, we were told.

It was during one of our afternoon story-writing exercises under the guidance of this seasoned professional journalist that I received the first indication that I was indeed beginning to make some progress.

We all lined up with our stories and, as so often happened when Bert put all those red lines in Biro through my copy, my fellow students were getting pretty much the same treatment.

At last, I reached the front of the queue and put my offering down on the desk in front of him and waited with bated breath as he quickly scanned through it with red Biro poised.

But amazingly, it never descended onto the page, not even once. Then to my utter surprise, he looked up at me and said: "You are a sub's dream."

All those endless hours I had spent, often late into the night, almost sweating blood, while trying to write parish council copy that Bert would not cover with red ink had, it seemed, at last paid off.

I and several others stayed in a B&B on the Cowbridge Road run by a Mr and Mrs Bowes and my one enduring memory of that time is tucking into bacon and eggs while listening to Radio Two and Peter Sarstedt singing: "Where do you go to my lovely when you are alone in your bed, tell me the thoughts that surround you because I want to get inside your head."

I think that record was Top of the Pops for the whole time we were in Cardiff and if ever I hear that hit song, I am instantly transported back to breakfast time with Mr and Mrs Bowes.

The dreaded Proficiency Test, which I simply had to pass to become a senior journalist, was looming like a dull toothache and I took mine on a grey and dreary day in Plymouth, having trundled down on the train the previous afternoon with a fellow junior from the Weston Mercury.

After a sleepless night in some basic B&B, we duly presented ourselves at the test centre, which I think was then the offices of the Plymouth Herald and the Western Morning News.

As part of the tests, candidates had to interview a fire chief on a one-to-one basis and he opened the proceedings by reading a short statement, which set the scene of an incident, but left out huge amounts of often critically-important information.

We each had a set time to ask all the right questions in order to extract the full story, before rushing off to a typewriter to produce our copy under deadline conditions.

Then it was off to another room to listen to a council meeting speech, take notes and produce still more copy, while racing against the clock.

After lunch, there were the written papers to test our knowledge of local government and the law and it was all over around 4pm.

I came out feeling drained and not over confident of the result, but still a lot better then that particularly memorable day when I had trailed around St Andrew's School playground listening to my far brighter friends discussing their answers to 11-Plus examination questions, which had been a total mystery to me!

When I later learnt that I had failed one of the sections and would have to retake it again, I was not overly surprised and, in fact, quite relieved that at least I was almost there.

I overcame the final qualification hurdle at the offices of the South Wales Echo and Western Mail in Cardiff on a day when it rained cats and dogs and satisfied my self- esteem by remembering that at least this was a 100 per cent improvement on my driving test record, which I passed on the fourth attempt!

One not-to-be missed highlight of those early years was the annual Christmas party held at the Clevedon Court, the mansion home of our proprietors.

Everyone employed at the Mercury, both on the editorial and Clevedon Printing Company side, was invited, as were all those employed on the Elton family's Clevedon Court Estate.

While our Editor was in charge of the free bar, his wife Joan, later to become the paper's photographer, was in charge of leading all the party games.

Besides the opening of the first Severn Bridge by the Queen and the building of the M5 across the North Somerset landscape, there were two other milestone stories that were to provide local journalists with thousands of column inches for years to come.

The first was the historic transatlantic return of the SS Great Britain, the world's first iron ship, to its birthplace in the Bristol City Docks, and the second was the development of the tiny North Somerset village of Nailsea into a large commuter town.

When I joined the Mercury, the village population was around 3,000, but all that was to change when county planners, under Government pressure to provide more housing land, decided it should be grown by phases into sizeable town.

Nailsea, protected then by the jealously-guarded Bristol and Bath Green Belt, was a comparatively quiet little place centred around its High Street, the village green, Silver Street and Clevedon Road.

There was the usual collection of quiet country pubs and fittingly, the largest employer was the Coates Cider factory, with its familiar collection of green-painted buildings at the Bristol end of the village.

"Coates comes up from Somerset where the Cider Apples Grow," ran its fondly- remembered advertising slogan.

Opposite the factory was the flower show field, where I spent many a summer hour collecting results and looking for stories, often fighting off a drowsiness caused by the canvas-induced heat, the heady scent of hundreds of blooms and too many late nights covering council meetings.

Nailsea too had its collection of characters, sadly now only memories, but who were all extremely kind and helpful to this callow young reporter.

There was the ebullient Arthur Davey, a staunch Royal British Legion supporter, who ran the Blue Iris coach firm and an undertaking business in Clevedon Road and Harry Wyatt, the local Somerset County Councillor, who would often give me lifts down to the meetings at County Hall in Taunton, where I was amused to see that all the members took in bottles of beer and packets of sandwiches.

Two of my other Nailsea favourites were local councillors, Cliff Bougourd, and Joe Stokes.

Both Cliff, who ran a green grocery in Silver Street, and Joe, a local market gardener, were members of the Long Ashton Rural District Council, where much of the development of Nailsea drama was to unfold, and they could always be relied upon for a telling quote.

Nailsea, county planners soon revealed, was to have, a new shopping centre, built around a piazza, a hexagonal library, a special water feature, a new road structure and, of course, hundreds of homes.

It was all grist to the mill for me because all this development was bound to generate literally hundreds of stories like fat and juicy apples, just waiting to be plucked from one of Coates' well-laden cider orchard trees.

One of the main news highlights of 1970, was the towing of the SS Great Britain on a giant pontoon up the Bristol Channel past Clevedon and Portishead.

Isambard Kingdom Brunel had built his steam-driven liner, the largest and most revolutionary ship of the age in 1843, to sail the North Atlantic as a sea-going extension of his Great Western Railway from London to Bristol.

But after a chequered career, she ended up as a rusting hulk in the Falkland Islands.

Thanks to a £150,000 donation from a millionaire philanthropist, Sir 'Union Jack' Hayward, and the tireless efforts of an enthusiastic band of preservationists, this most historic of ships, was eventually craned onto a giant floating pontoon and towed back across the Atlantic to her home port of Bristol.

I joined other reporters, cameramen and a large crowd on Portishead's Battery Point one early morning in June 1970 to watch the historic home-coming.

But while the ship's return had been known months in advance, there was another historic event waiting to happen, just over the horizon, that would provide me with a rich base cargo of stories for many years to come.

For while I was sitting in my usual position on the Press bench at long Ashton magistrates' Court at 10.20 am on the sunny morning of Friday, October 16th, Clevedon's Victorian pier suffered a partial collapse during safety weight tests.

Heavy duty plastic containers were filled with water and laid along the pier to create a pressure of 50ibs per square foot, but suddenly a weakness in one of the slender legs of the seventh span caused it to collapse, dragging the eighth and final span down into the water with it.

This historic amenity, opened amidst much rejoicing by the proud town's folk and with a parade of band and a cannon volley by the First Somerset Artillery in March, 1869, now lay in watery ruins.

Yet this feat of Victorian engineering with its slender arched spans made of Barlow rails from South Wales had until that time withstood all that the rampages of the second highest tide in the world could throw at it for just over 101 years.
"I only touched it with my coracle," a fun-loving Welshman, who ran a local café, remarked to Mervyn, who had nipped down from our offices in nearby Six Ways and was one of the first on the scene.

It was perhaps an attempt to make light of an incident that was now sending shockwaves across the town.

I continued following the court proceedings blissfully unaware of what had happened, because this was in the days long before mobile phones and I did not possess a bleeper used to alert photographers to call their news desks.

By 7pm that evening, a large and sombre crowd began gathering outside the Clevedon Council House, because word had gone quickly around that an emergency meeting was to be held.
"Why are you all here?" I asked. It was an incredibly stupid question, but in that moment, I could not think of anything else.

"We are here for the pier," replied a local, called, Mike Hedger, destined to become one of a small band of supporters, who would go on working tirelessly to save the pier for many years to come.

While there was the official version as to why the pier had actually collapsed, alternative theories abounded - two being that the water containers had been overfilled or that they were not filled quite enough, so that the minute the decking began leaning many more gallons of water had placed excessive weight on the weakened leg of the span.

The counter argument was that visitors suddenly running from one side of the pier to the other, as they followed the progress of a speed boat, would have had a similar effect and with disastrous consequences.

The pier was now a regular item on the council's agendas and the next milestone came when the town's engineer reported that repairs were expected to cost £75,000.

Oh, what a far cry that was to be from the around £2 million that had actually been spent by the time the pier was officially reopened in May 1998.

The pieces I wrote about the pier's collapse and the historic return of the SS Great Britain, formed part of my entry for the Young Journalist of the West award, made annually by the National Union of Journalists.

Mervyn, a staunch NUJ man, had often been keen that I should accompany him to the branch meetings, held with Weston Mercury colleagues over a pint at The Imperial Hotel in Weston on the occasional Saturday morning.

Having worked almost every day from 9am until 10pm because of the endless evening parish council meetings, the last thing I really wanted to do was to give up even the occasional precious Saturday morning, especially if it was summer time and I would be off to cover flower shows, carnivals, and fetes in the afternoon.

But being a member of the NUJ gave me my coveted Press card and I did not like to let Mervyn down, so I usually went along.

It was he who encouraged me to enter the Young Journalist of the West competition, so I made up a book containing the SS Great Britain home-coming and other examples of my work, including a story about some children from the village of Kingston Seymour, who discovered an unexploded wartime bomb out on the mud flats.

The winner was to be announced at a regional function at historic Longleat House, Lord Bath's magnificent stately home in Wiltshire.

The competition, it appeared, had been entered by dozens of young journalists from five counties and it had taken the judges in London and Cheltenham eight hours to select the top male and female entries.

Driving the Mercury Minivan, I followed Mervyn and his wife, Dorothy, along endless country lanes on a dark and very wet night with him stopping every few hundred yards to wipe his windscreen because his wipers had packed up.

I began wondering, if he really did know the way and whether we would ever get there and when we did eventually arrive, we found the well-attended function in full swing in one of the sumptuous banqueting rooms.

There was a generous buffet supper, after which the awards were announced, and to my complete and utter surprise, the male winner turned out to be me.

Still in a bit of a daze, I was presented with a cheque for £12.50 by the NUJ National President and a bright orange portable typewriter, handed over by Lord Bath.

Later that evening, I was approached by Keith Jefferies, then News Editor of our biggest rival, the Bristol Evening Post, who offered me a district reporting job covering my North Somerset patch.

It was customary for a young journalist to move on to a daily paper once he or she had obtained the coveted Proficiency Certificate, so that a new apprentice could be indentured.

But I had somehow become Chief Reporter when Mervyn had taken over the Sub-editor's role, after Bert's eventual retirement, and I had never been encouraged to leave, so what was I to do?

The paper had taken on another junior, but she had not worked out, so it was just Mervyn and I running the show with the help of a long-serving team of freelances.

These included a by then, quite elderly, Grace Sawden, who covered Portishead and wrote a weekly column full of local interest, called Posset Pie, and, Gray Usher, our very long-serving agricultural correspondent who, the former very junior me, would occasionally accompany on his round of gossip-seeking farm visits.

So just what was I to do about this tempting offer of joining the Bristol Evening Post, with the added benefit, and indeed comfort, of covering North Somerset in direct opposition to Mervyn and all at the South Avon Mercury?

It was quite nice being a larger fish in an extremely small pond and I was not hurrying to give Keith and answer.

But, one afternoon, he called up and put me right on the spot, so 20 agonising minutes later, I nipped out to the telephone box opposite the office, called him back, and accepted.

JOINING THE BRISTOL EVENING POST

It was agreed by Keith, and Editor, Gordon Farnsworth, that I should spend a couple of weeks in the Bristol Head Office, learning the ropes, before being given a staff Mini car and send out to cover North Somerset, while working from home.

I had not long married and home for my wife, Wendy, and I was a prefabricated holiday bungalow owned by a friend's mother in Nore Road, Portishead.

Entering, what I seem to remember was a four-storey red brick, building in Silver Street, close to the city fire station, I took the lift, up to the editorial floor and made by way over to Keith, who was occupying the all-important News Desk.

It was the epicentre of the entire news-gathering operation, which back in those heady days, covered a considerable area of the South-west with district offices in neighbouring Gloucestershire, Wiltshire, and Somerset, shared with the sister newspaper, the Western Daily Press, known as the WDP.

Phones were ringing and typewriters were clattering away, with some 20 reporters busy working on range of stories for the One Star and its slip local news editions, being prepared for production and despatch, by a whole fleet of delivery vans around noon.

The race was then on to see whether it would be the Bristol Evening Post, or the Liverpool Echo, who would be the first to reach a 200,000 daily circulation.

An invisible line down one side of the room, separated the busy Post news gathering team from that of their smaller group of WDP rivals, whose desks were mostly empty, because they worked from early afternoon until late into the evening.

Oh, what a contrast this busy evening paper newsroom was with our quiet and cosy little set-up in Clevedon.

Still, if all went well, then in a couple of weeks, I would be able to escape back to my familiar and comfortable little world.

And that, being honest with myself, is what I have been doing mostly all my life - putting my head over the parapet, but always arranging things, so that I can quickly retreat to the safety of my comfort zone.

Yet when I have summoned up the courage to break new ground, fortune has usually favoured me.

There was a tangible sense of feverish activity in that busy newsroom on that first and on subsequent mornings.

I was given a desk and asked to complete a quick rewrite of a piece that had just appeared in the WDP, which had to be turned around well before the first 9.30 am deadline.

As at the Mercury, we wrote our copy on small sheets of blank newsprint paper, putting each of the first three introduction paragraphs on separate sheets and then following on with the rest of the story, written three or four "pars" per sheet.

But we needed a copy or black of each story, so two sheets were used with a sheet of carbon paper in between.

The blacks were kept as a record of a story, in case of queries later on, and also sometimes passed on to the WDP.

This system made life easier for the sub-editors, who were seated around a large table on the floor below.

Completed copy was presented to the News Editor, who quickly scanned it, and, if satisfied, would commit it to a small cylindrical container and send it whizzing on its way down to the subs table, in a high-pressure air-operated Lamson Tube.

This probably now long-forgotten system was also used by the big Debenhams and John Lewis department stores across the way in the then-thriving Broadmead shopping complex.

Here, till operators used it to send over cash and invoices to a finance department, while customers waited for their change and receipts to be returned.

Digressing for a moment, I vividly remember the five-year-old me sitting upstairs on a green double decker bus in the 1950s and driving past a massive construction site, which was Broadmead in the making.

So back in the newsroom, after I had completed my rewrite well before the 9.30am deadline, and as a new boy on his first day, I was transferred to the far less pressurised Country Desk,

Here I spent the remainder of my time writing stories, which were going on 'overnight pages, for the following day's country slip editions.

A small gratifying incident that occurred many years after I had left the Post and launched my own small news PR operation, has just slipped into my mind, so although it rather borders on being embarrassingly self-contratulatory, I will mention it here.

I had been tasked to produce a tabloid-style quarterly newspaper for a client, so enlisted the valuable assistance of a former Evening Post sub-editor to put headlines on my stories and complete the lay out and instructions for the printers.

"When a new person joined us on the sub's table, we always started him off on Nigel Heath copy because that was easy to sub," he told me, while we were working together one morning.

Instantly the comment made by that Birmingham Mail tutor on our journalist course in Cardiff some years earlier, sprang to mind, but becoming a 'sub's dream' had, as you may recall, only come after many painful months of me striving not to have Bert's red biro all over my fledgling copy.

While I was busy working away on the Country Desk, close by a team of lady copytakers, headphones clamped to their ears, were busy typing out even more stories, being phoned in by district reporters and freelances, either working from home or standing in red telephone boxes all around the region.

These were the heady days before local radio and television, when the regional morning and evening newspapers were the only source of immediate local news.

People would queue for their paper outside Evening Post district offices in towns, like Clevedon, while special machines printed the very latest sports results on to a space deliberately left blank on the back page.

The next juicy instalments from long-running Bristol court cases would be avidly awaited night after night, as would the latest news from an important public inquiry, or a hunt for a robber or rapist.

Journalists working on all these stories would either nip out to a public telephone to file their update pieces over to the copytakers or hurry back to the offices to bash out their words.

Bristol's Crown and County Courts were nearby, so a messenger would walk across at regular intervals to collect the latest copy from the Post's Court Reporter, who spent his or her time, almost entirely on court reporting.

If there happened to be a particular sensational case being heard in the Crown Court, then the Post 'staffer' would most probably be joined by regional journalists working for all the 'nationals.

Also in attendance in court for important cases, or on the scene of any big or breaking story would be a reporter from the Press Association, whose reports were then syndicated widely to all the nationals and regional papers across the country, which subscribed to its services.

It really was a exciting time to be in newspapers because a reporter could literally be first with the news and the best and most satisfying reward would be one's by-line under a bold black and sensational headline.

I discovered later, on my first day that the Post's shipping and motoring reporter, Dave Baxter, lived only a mile away from me and he kindly agreed to come and pick me up each morning until I got my own wheels.

I had no way of knowing it then, but Dave was to join me many years later after I had left the Post and launched my own fledgling news PR operation.

It was a meeting of the Long Ashton Rural District Council's Planning Committee at The Grange, in the village of Flax Bourton, that looked set to give me my first opportunity of writing to meet immediate deadlines.

I had already covered many of these sessions as a Mercury reporter, but this was to be my first real experience of working under pressure.

I had now taken possession of a new bright orange Mini car for my new "patch" of North Somerset, but was still attached to head office and was therefore send out from Bristol to cover the proceedings.

Councillors were all in their seats by 10am and the opening items concerned a boring old house extension, followed by a barn conversion and an equally dull new house plan.

There were no wrecks and nobody 'drownded,' in fact and nothing to laugh at, at all, I thought thinking back to my childhood days when my Mum would recite the famous Stanley Holloway music hall monologue about Albert and the Lion.

But the situation was not at all funny because after scanning all the applications, I quickly realised councillors were unlikely to reach the only interesting item on the agenda until I was on deadline, especially if they went on making an absolute meal of every issue.

The Long Ashton planners were normally pretty good at getting through the business, but today of all days, they seemed to have got it into their heads to be in no particular hurry.
If I had still been reporting for the Mercury, it would not have mattered a jot, but now it did matter, it mattered a lot!

My heart began to thump. To fail on my first assignment was unthinkable, especially as copy from this meeting was usually needed to fill some holes in my own local North Somerset edition.

Normally one could rely on at least three reasonable pieces coming up in the first hour, but today it looked like it was going to be different.

The one and only story with some potential was a retrospective application for yet another house extension.

The applicants had obviously started building without permission and now wanted the council to approve of their work, so that it could continue.

If councillors said "no," then they would have to take the extension down and that would certainly be a story.

I waited and hoped against hope for a decent controversy, with maybe a petition from angry neighbours, and watched the hands of the clock move ever closer to my 11.30am deadline.

Councillors eventually reached the item at just after 11.20am and I got ready for some speedy note taking.

"This is a very minor infringement, Mr Chairman," began one of the council's Planning Officers.

"This extension was only at foundation stage when it was spotted and all is in order except, of course, for the lack of an application."

The committee chairman nodded. "Does the Parish Council have any observations?" he asked. They too, it seemed, were happy and there was even a letter of support from the immediate neighbours.

Blast! I thought, leaving my seat, and going off to use the telephone. "Absolutely nothing doing here, not even a half reasonable overnight piece," I reported to Keith.

He must have detected the disappointment in my voice. "Not to worry. The paper's tight now anyway, so you might as well come back," he told me.

I felt a surge of relief as I walked through the park-like grounds to my lovely new and shiny Mini. A wintery sun was shining and I lived to fight another day.

It was on my last Saturday shift in the office before going off to work from home that I got my first ever by-line story.

But ironically, it gave me no pleasure because it was a result of a reader's pain and graphically demonstrated how it takes only a telephone call to plunge a reporter into the midst of a human crisis or tragedy.

The lady, whose call I picked up, was crying and talking to me between sobs, so it was difficult to make out quite what she was saying, but the conversation went something like this:

"How can they do this?" she told me. "Do what?" I asked sympathetically. "Invite him to London and roll out the red carpet," she replied.

Again, she was sobbing, so I waited a moment. "Invite whom?" I asked gently.

"That terrorist Menachem Begin." She replied. "What did he do?" I asked? "He murdered my brother."

Begin was beginning his first visit to London as the new Israeli Prime Minister, yet in 1945 and 1946 he had led the Irgun terrorist organisation, which launched an offensive against British rule in Palestine with a wave of bomb attacks and the blowing up of the King David Hotel in Jerusalem, which killed 90 people.

This poor lady's brother had been one of the ten British soldiers, who had lost their lives during that offensive – hanged from lamp-posts.

The following Monday morning found me setting up my office at home in Portishead and beginning a daily routine that was to last for the next 17 years.

I have always taken a morning walk, normally leaving home between 5.45am and 6.30am and the last port of call from the very beginning of my Evening Post days, was always the newsagents to pick up a WDP.

I would read it from cover to cover over breakfast, slowly turning the pages and always hoping not to find a story from my patch that I knew nothing about.

If I had been 'scooped,' then I would spend a hectic thirty minutes on the typewriter and telephone, hurriedly trying to find a fresh angle, and rewriting the story for our first edition.
Luckily this did not happen too often and I could usually close the paper with the words always said aloud: "Well, nothing to worry about there then."

It was a familiar refrain that I am sure that my now, long grown up, children, Natalie and Robin, will remember, as we sat around our small breakfast table.

In fact in following years, when I regularly scooped the WDP, its Assistant Editor, Peter Gibbs, later to become a colleague, friend and long-distance walking companion, would refer to me as "the blasted Heath."

My call-in time was 8.15am and I would tell Keith, or whoever happened to be manning the news desk that morning, what I had planned for the day.

Thanks to a diary follow-up system, which I adopted from day one, there were only three or four occasions over the whole of my time with the Evening Post, when I had to say there was simply nothing about.

It worked on the principle that for every story, there is always a follow-up, so whenever I wrote a piece, I would always made a diary note to revisit it in anything from a week to six months later.

Given that I normally turned out between four and eight different pieces every day, my diary soon reached the point where there were several follow-up items to look at every morning.

My first daily tasks, if I was not busy on a rewrite from the Western Daily Press, were always my routine calls to the police and the ambulance service to find out what had been happening overnight.

Hourly calls to the Avon and Somerset Fire Brigade were always handled by head office and I was quickly contacted if there was a blaze on my patch.

It was to be a fire related incident that was to give me a great story from a Clevedon Urban District Council meeting, soon after I started working from home and this was to more than make up for my dismal failure at the hands of the Long Ashton planners, although it was a close-run thing.

The Clevedon Council House, on Highdale Road, was a significant Georgian mansion with tremendous views over the town and its large and lofty first floor council chamber was fittingly a room of some grandeur.

This evening committee meeting opened with me looking out expectantly on a row of by now very familiar faces and then beginning to flick through the agenda, minutes and supporting papers, looking out for any item which might give me a story.

There were none, so I went through more slowly and carefully a second time, as Council Clerk, John Billington, launched into the formalities with apologies for absence and the minutes of the last meeting. 'I don't believe this,' I thought.

'There is really nothing of any significance here at all, a few filler pars maybe, but nothing that's going to produce even one half-reasonable piece. Was this to be a repeat of last week?'

To come away from one meeting without a story was bad enough, but two in a row was unthinkable.

Rain lashed the windows, and the proceedings dragged on with one lengthy discussion after another on matters that were really of no particular interest to anyone, and then I noticed it.

Curled up snakelike and half visible under one of the tables near the window end of the chamber was a rope!

What on earth was that doing there? I stared at it and the more I looked, the more puzzling it seemed to be and I began to experience that funny little sensation, a sort of rising excitement, which I get when I sense that I am on to something.
I had now lost all interest in the dreary proceedings and could not wait for them to be over, so that I might solve this mystery.

When at last the members had dispensed with any other business and began gathering up their papers and chatting, I approached the clerk.

"John what is that rope doing under there?" I asked.

"Oh! I was rather hoping that nobody would notice it because it's our temporary fire escape," he replied.

"What do you mean?" I asked incredulously.

It turned out there had been an Avon and Somerset Fire Brigade routine inspection earlier in the day and the council chamber was declared to be at risk because the exterior fire escape was found to be dangerously unsafe.

"We were advised to provide the rope purely as a temporary measure, until emergency repairs can be made," he said.

"But it must be at least fifteen metres to the ground and most of the councillors are getting on a bit, so do you really think they could use it?" I asked.

"Well, you had better ask them," he replied, and that is just what I did and what a great story it turned out to be!

Life settled down into a comfortable routine with me covering the urban and rural council meetings in Clevedon, Portishead and Flax Bourton and attending Long Ashton Magistrates' Court on Fridays, much as I had done for the Mercury.

I can still see many of the friendly faces that looked toward the Press table from three semi-circular rows of chairs, and up to the dais behind me, where their appropriate committee chairman, or woman, and the officers sat, for meetings of the very progressive, Long Ashton Rural District Council.

Their offices were in a small mansion called, The Grange, set in large gardens in the village of Flax Bourton and their council and committee meetings were mostly always held in the mornings.

I described this now long defunct, local authority as progressive, because it was run along non-party lines and went ahead to get got things done.

I usually managed to pop out of the meetings and file at least three or four stories for that afternoon's North Somerset edition by the noon deadline.

I achieved this by writing up the first piece, while keeping an ear open and scribbling down short and suitable quotes from the following item of interest on the agenda, and so on.

The then Rector of the nearby hillside village of Wraxall, was always good for a quote because he would he would refer to items in ecclesiastical terms and say, for example: "This site would be as big as a cathedral!"

Then there was the member for, I think it was North Weston, who would always refer to the 'beautiful Gordano Valley,' which was an area of farmland between wooded hills.

It was pleasant enough, but hardly beautiful, considering that the M5 now ran all along one side of it!

I lost count of the times over the years that this lovely man got to his feet and prefaced his remarks with the opening phrase: "Mr Chairman; I am a little bit disturbed!"

A story that was definitely not on this council's agenda came right out of the blue, one lunch time when, having just driven away from the meeting, I spotted one of their middle-aged lady employees waiting at a nearby bus stop, so stopped and offered her a lift.

"Have you got a half day off?" I asked when we were on the move again.

"Oh no. I have got to get home because my husband called me in the office to tell me that the bailiffs have just turned up to evict us from our council house!"

I drove her straight home and wasted no time in calling the council with the news that they were in the process of making one of their own staff homeless! Needless to say, the eviction was halted.

Working for the Post with its thrice-daily, rather than weekly deadlines, kept me very much on my toes and a point came when to save time, I found myself being able to think up the intro sentence and then dictate the rest of the story over the phone to the copy takers, straight out of my notebook.

If there had been a fatal road accident overnight, the news desk needed my story within a couple of hours at the most.

If a road victim's name had been released by the police, then I would be sent hot-foot to interview the next of kin.

I would turn up on the doorstep, part of me hoping that whoever answered, would tell me not to intrude on their grief and to go away, but this hardly ever happened.

They were always in a state of shock and unreality and in that space would invite me in and invariably offer me a cup of tea.

While they were going through the motions of making it, I would be calmly scanning the room for any picture of the victim, which I might borrow, and also glancing at my watch, to see just how much time I now had to do the interview before heading for the nearest phone box to put over my story.

It sounds terribly cold and calculating, but all that former experience of calling up widows and widowers to write obituaries for the Mercury, seemed to have de-sensitised me and allowed me to view these unhappy situations with a certain amount of detachment.

I invariably found that people simply wanted to talk about their loved ones, while still finding it difficult to accept that they had gone for ever.

I could always identify with that terrible feeling of unreality by remembering back to that awful bleak February afternoon when my dear Mum came through the door and told my brother, sister, and I that Daddy had gone to Jesus. I was thirteen at the time.

He had collapsed with a cerebral haemorrhage earlier that morning at our home then in Clevedon's Kings Road at the upper end of the town.

There were inevitably occasions when my defences were pierced by a terrible tragedy-- like the time I had to report on the death of a young man on the day before his wedding.

There were also many times when I would be in the middle of one rush story when another would suddenly break to give me a double dose of adrenalin.

By lunch times the panics were almost always over and I could relax a bit and start thinking about writing up some overnight pieces for the following day's paper, but it was not always the case.

Not long after Wendy and I had moved into a three-bedroom linked detached property in Park Road, Congresbury, I got a 1.30pm call from the office to say that a farm house was on fire just off the A370 Bristol to Weston-super-Mare Road.

I was told that if I was quick, they could probably squeeze a couple of 'pars' into our Three Star edition.

Abandoning my lunch, I leapt into by office Mini and could see the smoke rising somewhere ahead as I sped out of the village.

The Fire Brigade from nearby Yatton had already arrived and were busy tackling a substantial blaze in the roof.

Farm hands were moving animals and machinery out of adjoining buildings and a woman, whom I took to be the farmer's wife, was simply standing and watching the spectacle, tears pouring down her face.

But in the midst of this frenzied activity, I spotted four young men, not in uniform, who were busy running around checking hose connections and making themselves generally useful.

'That's a bit odd,' I thought, but then took no further notice of them as I endeavoured to get enough information for my copy, without getting in the way or hindering the fire-fighting operation.

With just a few minutes to spare before the final deadline of the day, I sped further on down the A370, because I knew there was a telephone box in the next village and, thankfully, it had not been vandalised, or otherwise, out of order.

These distinctive red cast-iron structures, designed by Sir Giles Gilbert Scott, architect of Liverpool Cathedral and Battersea Power Station, among other notable buildings, were our vital link to head office in the days before mobile phones.

But when I turned to come out, I was stopped dead in my tracks by the most bizarre sight. There were those young men, whom I had spotted earlier, walking towards me pushing a miniature fire engine.

"Look lads just tell me what's going on?" I asked. "You won't believe this," one of them replied, "but we are Birmingham firemen on a sponsored fire appliance push to Weston-super-Mare in aid of our benevolent fund," he explained.

"And, yes," broke in one of his friends, "we were the first on the scene of this blaze and all we had was a toy fire engine and a two-foot ladder!"

I went straight back into the phone box and called up a photographer, who managed to catch up with them a few miles further long the road.

There were to be a number of occasions along my career highway when fact turned out to be stranger or funnier than fiction and this was definitely one of them.

But fire can be a terrible calamity and I have stood in the blackened ruins of enough homes to be almost paranoid about removing plugs from all but the most essential electrical appliances before going out.

THE SWISS AIR DISASTER

I had been covering my North Somerset patch for the Post, just over three years, when I popped into the chemist's shop in my home village of Congresbury around 4pm on an April evening for some now long forgotten reason.

"I suppose you've heard the news," remarked Derek Cox, our friendly and always most helpful pharmacist. "What news is that, Derek?" I asked.

"I've just heard there's been a terrible accident involving that shopping flight to Basle that took off from Bristol Airport this morning," he replied.

Within hours it was confirmed that almost 140 people, mainly mothers, had boarded an Invicta Airlines flight for a day's shopping and sightseeing in Basle and that the plane had come down.

But at that early stage, no one knew just how serious the situation was and it only emerged much later that the plane had struck the tops of trees and crashed into a wooded hillside on its second attempt to land at the Swiss airport, in the midst of a snow storm.

The flight was the third annual outing for members of the Axbridge Ladies' Guild, who had been accompanied by members of the Mum's Night Out Group, from nearby Cheddar, and skittles players from Congresbury and the neighbouring village of Wrington.

Axbridge, was just over the border in my colleague, John Barber's, patch, but he lived in Weston and was not around at the time.

So, I drove over the Mendip Hills and down into this historic little Somerset town, the smallest in the county, which was clearing going to be the epicentre as far as news gathering for this terrible story.

It would be several weeks before I learned that among the 108, who died, were twenty Congresbury villagers, including two children, Bill Price, my 'lonely and out of work undertaker' and his wife, Dorothy, and May Atwell, to whom I was related and who had served me many a drink from behind her tiny bar in The Plough Inn.

It is quite difficult to describe the scene I encountered on entering the historic square, now more than fifty years ago, other than it resembled the peace before the storm, with people walking about in a daze and talking quietly together in small groups.

I may well have been the first reporter on the scene and it soon became clear that everyone I spoke to was waiting for news as to whether their loved ones had survived or had lost their lives.

It was pointless taking notes from individuals before they knew what had happened to their close family members, so I just did my best to describe what I had experienced before driving home with a heavy heart.

I spoke earlier about the calm before the storm and the storm, to which I as referring, was the one which broke early the following morning, when the entire national media circus rolled into town and began pointing their cameras and microphones into bewildered people's faces.

My national media colleagues, most of whom were responsible and empathetic journalists, were only doing their jobs.

But it was the sheer volume of the intrusion that very quickly became so overwhelming that many of the, at first bemused, locals, simply wished they'd all pack up, go away and leave them to grieve.

The Post's highly-experienced Aviation Correspondent, Malcolm Smith, flew out to the town of Hotchwold near the crash site to cover the story as it unfolded day by day, with the survivors being treated in hospital and grieving relatives having to fly out to identify their loved ones.

Meanwhile, my colleague John, took over reporting the story locally and I was not at all sorry at withdrawing from the scene, but was sent out to Bristol Airport some weeks later to cover the late evening arrival of a flight carrying all the survivors.

I can still see the aircraft in my mind's eye after it came to a standstill not far away on the floodlit runway and the steps were run out and the door opened, but no one emerged.

Then the news came that the passengers were refusing to leave the aircraft until all the reporters and camera crews had withdrawn.

By this time, the Evening Post had vacated its rabbit warren of offices opposite the old fire station in Silver Street and had moved into a brand-new print centre in nearby Temple Way.

The paper changed its format from a tabloid to a broadsheet. "We are letting our tail down," the paper boldly announced, but the move was against the national trend and the Post lost thousands of sales almost overnight and never recovered them.

My wife and I had just invested the huge sum of £90 in some beige-coloured curtains with an arty green reed-like pattern to hang inside our front door, when I was suddenly summoned into the office for a meeting called by the National Union of Journalists.

National negotiations for a substantial pay rise had been dragging on for weeks and had finally broken down, so now we were out on strike.

It was getting close to Christmas, the weather was turning much colder and prospects were looking decidedly bleak.

'It was a godsend that we still had one income coming in, but I wished we had not bought those curtains,' I thought as I drove slowly back to Congresbury late on a lovely sunny morning.

Support for the strike was almost 100 per cent, so we were all in the same boat.

A picket line was set up at the rear goods entrance to the building and one resourceful journalist brought along a small caravan, which we parked on a nearby patch of grass belonging to the company.

Thinking back on it now, it's surprising that the management never ordered us to move it.

An old oil drum doubled as a brazier, which we kept alight mainly with bits of pallets purloined from a nearby trading estate.

Everyone took turns at being on picket duty in groups of three or four and I spent a miserable Boxing Day afternoon being either freezing cold or alternately singed from standing too close to our fire.

The paper continued to appear in a much-reduced form being produced by management with the aid of news agency copy and a scattering of journalists and some freelances, who were still working.

As the weeks dragged on with no resolution in sight, the dispute became more and more bitter - those driving into work were given a very hard time by jeering pickets and there were some ugly confrontations, exacerbated by militants drawn to the scene from elsewhere in the country.

I got a part-time job on the petrol pumps at a garage in Portishead and began doing various decorating jobs for relations.

Just what was my life coming too, I began to wonder, but there was light at the end of the tunnel and after nine long weeks, it was eventually over and we had gained a sizeable pay rise.

Every year, amateur dramatic groups from right across our circulation area would compete for the Post's coveted Rose Bowl trophy.

I seem to recall that the judges attended these performances anonymously, but that a reporter would always go along on one evening to write a short review for his or her local edition.

Most towns and villages across my North Somerset patch had their am-dram enthusiasts, so come the season, I would have to spend at least one night a week covering these plays.

I have to say, that most of the acting by these enthusiastic amateurs was generally of a high standard, because many of them had been treading the boards for years, so their performances were entertaining.

But when one had been on duty from 7.45am, the idea of driving out again at 6.30pm with the prospect of not getting home until around 11pm, was not altogether appealing.

So, I adopted a cunning plan and that was to slip in just as the curtain was about to rise, and provided, that I had managed to grab a programme and seen all the actors, then to slip out again in the interval.

It was a slightly risky strategy because if the community hall, where most of these shows were staged, happen to catch fire or, God forbid, an actor collapse on stage, then I would have some explaining to do.

Luckily this never happened to me, but when much-loved comedian Eric Morecambe collapsed and died on stage in Tewkesbury, Gloucestershire, the freelance, who was covering the performance for our WDP colleagues, did not bother to tell the paper, because she wrongly thought that the deadline had passed.

Anyway, my cunning plan would not work if I was recognised on arrival and ushered to my reserved seat at the front of the house and asked what drink I would like in the interval.

On one memorable occasion, I took my mother along to watch three one act plays at the Clevedon Community Centre and, as I had an elderly lady on my arm, I was not recognised, which turned out to be a blessing.

As it happened to be a cold winter's night, all the hall's heaters, which at that time were suspended from the lofty ceiling on rods, were on full blast.

I had had a tiring day and as the dialogue was not particularly stimulating, we both closed our eyes and drifted off to sleep and managed to miss the second and much shorter play completely.

There was only one course of action open to me now, and that was to be complimentary to all the actors in that play.

But having said that, I was no theatre critic and as these performers were all enthusiastic amateurs, who was I to make anything other than positive observations about them all.

It was around this time that the Avon and Somerset Constabulary began sending their Community Constables to parish council meetings to report on crime prevention and other relevant local matters.

Covering these evening meetings was always a bit of a chore especially if one had already been on duty since 8.15am, so I tended to only go to the more important ones and to those, where I knew in advance that some newsworthy issue was on the agenda.

So it was that I went along to a meeting of Winford Parish Council, being held for a change in nearby Regil Village Hall.

Local opposition to further expansion at Bristol Airport was gathering momentum and this was to be a particularly important meeting.

Our rivals, the WDP, had decided to send along their own reporter, rather than relying on copy which would normally have been supplied by me under a reciprocal agreement, because, after all, both papers were part of Bristol United Press.

I took my place on the table set aside for the Press and spotted my rival come in and choose a seat in the body of the room.

I looked around the rapidly-filling hall and then saw a police Chief Inspector come in and sit himself down in the front row. What on earth has brought him here? I wondered.

The more I thought about it, the more convinced I became that something was up because Chief Inspectors did not normally attend parish council meetings and if he was a local, it was highly unlikely that he would have been in uniform, I reasoned.

Had the WDP reporter also spotted this obvious anomaly? I wondered. I knew he would be under some pressure to file his story and I just hoped he would leave once the airport item had been discussed.

The chairman took it first and as soon as it was over, quite a few of the locals, and the WDP man, slipped out.

I breathed a sigh of relief and settled down to write up my airport story and to wait for the very last agenda item, marked Local Police Report.

Luckily the members sped through the remainder of the business and I was then rewarded with one of the best stories to come out of a parish council meeting in years, and which made the airport controversy pale into insignificance.

The Chief Inspector's Community Constable and his family also happened to live in the village and some unknown individuals had started making their lives a misery with a series of stupid pranks, including letting down tyres, stealing milk and moving their dustbin at regular intervals.

The Chief Inspector said this vendetta had to be stopped forthwith and he appealed to villagers to help catch the culprits.

Not surprising the story made our Page One lead the next day and I could not help feeling sorry for that WDP man, who would almost certainly have got it in the neck from his News Editor for missing out.

PRESS TRIPS

Once every couple of years and right out of the blue a reporter would be asked by the news editor if he or she would like to go off on a Press trip, which was, in reality, a week's paid holiday.

These Press facilities were offered by tour operators and other travel companies keen to have their holidays reviewed in a favourable light in the nationals or in major regional newspapers like the Post.

There were normally between six and ten invitees representing publications across the country, and as our hosts were out to impress, one could generally be assured of having a good time.

But it could all become a little too much on some occasions and there was one particular trip, to Athens, Crete and Corfu, that springs to mind.

We landed in Athens and were met by our hosts, who whisked us off to our luxurious hotel for welcome drinks before we retired to our respective suites to freshen up.

By 11am we had all assembled in a conference suite for coffee and a welcome introduction by the local tourist board.

Then we were taken by coach to visit a resort hotel where a sumptuous buffet lunch had been laid out, presided over by three chefs in their traditional 'whites.'

We were all quite peckish by now and soon had plates laden with traditional Greek fare.

Then it was back on the coach for short drive to another hotel where, after a tour, a sumptuous afternoon tea had been laid on.

Needless to say, no one was hungry, but it would have been churlish not to have made some half-hearted effort at sampling the fare.

We were back at our hotel by 5.45pm and all went to our rooms to rest and change prior to reassembling down in the bar for drinks followed by a gala dinner.

Alas, there was no time to rest, because by 10am the following morning, we were on a short flight to Crete, where scenic island tours, interspersed with yet more receptions, had been planned.

There were inevitable casualties from this hectic pace, including one journalist, who fell asleep in his bath which then overflowed.

Luckily there was some time to relax after we moved on to Corfu, where four of us hired a pedalo and voyaged out as far as we dared into the stretch of water between the island and Albania, which was pretty much a closed book back in those far off days.

Then there was the occasion, not long after I had joined the Post, when I was sent off on a charter flight from Bristol Airport to tour Rumania, accompanying 60 lady members of the paper's highly popular Women's Circle.

My abiding memory of our coach tour around a scenic country, then steeped in agriculture with horse drawn carts, was our late afternoon arrival in the capital, Bucharest.

Stupidly, I had managed to lose the key to my case and when the news quickly went around, an orderly queue of ladies assembled along the corridor outside my room with everyone keen to see if their key would fit my lock.

I was dubious after the first few failures and was beginning to think about what to do next, when as if by magic, my recalcitrant case opened!

When we all assembled for a buffet supper in the restaurant, we found a wedding reception in full swing just across the wide hallway in an old-fashioned ball room, dripping with chandeliers.

While all the men were in black suits, the women were waltzed around the floor in elaborate ball gowns that looked as if they had come from an earlier time.

The highlight of our tour was our visit to the central Transylvania region with its mountainous borders and fairy tale castles and, of course, we had to visit the picturesque Gothic Castle, linked to Count Dracula.

Our base for a couple of nights was the historic city of Brasov with its Saxon walls and bastions and magnificent central square ringed by cafes and colourful baroque buildings and towering Gothic Black Church, nearby.

Following a tour around the foothills of the Southern Carpathian Mountains it was time to turn around and go home.

If I had been given £10 for every story intro I wrote that began: Angry residents of such and such a village, I would have made a lot of money over the years.

It was not that people in my patch were a particularly belligerent lot, but I must have written hundreds of stories about people protesting about one thing or another.

One, particular protest I remember, brought the ladies of the Long Ashton Woman's Institute to national prominence and it centred around an oak tree at the Bristol end of the village.

The ancient oak had been condemned as dangerous and was due to be felled, but the ladies begged to differ and climbed up into its branches to prevent it being axed.

"We are not all jam and Jerusalem," one of the campaigners shouted down to me. Their highly publicised protest went on for several weeks before they eventually gave in and the tree was given the chop.

It had been the custom in earlier times to plant oaks at crossroads around the area and they must have all reached the end of their natural span around the same time, because I later wrote other sad stories about these lovely gnarled old trees being axed at Wraxall, Walton-in-Gordano and several other places, and then follow-up pieces on new ones being planted to take their places.

I gave the people of Flax Bourton a lot of coverage for their campaign to limit the speed of traffic through their village, so much so, that they invited me to open their annual summer fete.

I did not relish the honour, but it would have been churlish to have declined, so I duly arrived on a damp Saturday afternoon under leaden skies with lines of flags hanging limp and dripping, and made myself know to the organisers.

I was asked if I would first judge the Monsters Competition and ushered into a small tent, where I found a cluster of weird-looking creatures made of cardboard, tin cans or papier-mache and all neatly labelled and laid out on a trestle table ready for inspection.

I was in there for a little while and when I emerged the fete seemed to be in full swing without my having opened it, so I started wandering around the stalls and side shows.

'Thank goodness I no longer had to make lists of stallholders,' I said to myself, remembering back to my first summer on the Clevedon Mercury.

Then to my surprise, the lady, who had invited me to open the proceedings, came up and said that she had not actually heard my speech, but she expected it was very good.

I suddenly felt too embarrassed to admit that there had been no official opening and simply nodded.

Perhaps I could quietly slip away, I thought, but before I could do so, my host, who by now had discovered the terrible truth, came rushing up full of apologies and guided me, now rather reluctantly, towards a lonesome microphone set up on the other side of the field.

So it was that I probably became the first ever guest of honour to officially stop a summer fete in full swing only to start it again.

As I was covering North Somerset for the Post, I would make occasional use of its small office in Clevedon's Station Road, just around the corner from The Triangle Shopping centre with its magnificent stand-alone and Grade 11-listed, Victorian clock tower.

Here, Ray Mogg, would operate the heavy machine, which allowed him to roller out the very latest sports result onto a corresponding blank space on the back page of the paper. Those were the heady days when readers would form a queue along the pavement to buy their evening paper.

It was late one afternoon when I was sitting in a back room behind the sales counter, that I came across a story, which was to give me my first ever page one lead concerning the Port of Bristol.

For tucked away towards the end of a long list of planning applications, was one from Japanese car maker, Toyota, seeking permission for a big new car import and export facility, just along the Bristol Channel coast at the loss-making Royal Portbury Dock, which actually sat on my patch.

Sadly, the scheme did not proceed for one now long-forgotten reason or another, but while I could not have known it at the time, the dock did go on to become a major UK car handling terminal.

If I learned one important life lesson from all my years with the Bristol Evening Post, it was the amazing power of positive energy.

Time and time again, when up against a deadline, a door would suddenly and magically swing open, enabling me to succeed.

It was as if when I really put a huge amount of effort into tracking down someone for an urgently-needed quote or to 'stand up' a story then I would often win through against all the odds and in the nick of time.

Now I can hear the cynics and the realists among you thinking: "Well, that's obvious, because, of course, you are more likely to succeed if you put a lot of effort into something."

I can't and don't disagree with that, but what I do know and I have observed from years of experience, is that some amazing and quite coincidental things have happened far too often in these situations to be simply explained away as reward for effort.

One shining example was the morning I was asked by the news desk to try and get hold of a Frank Reynolds for an urgently-needed quote.

They believed he lived in the Walton area of Clevedon, but he was not answering his telephone, so could I follow it up from there. It was then just after 10am and they needed the quote by noon at the latest.

I tried the number they had given me just in case he might have come back in from the garden. No answer, so I reached for the bulky telephone directory, which in those days was an essential reference tool, but could find no F Reynolds in Clevedon, which meant that he was probably ex-directory.

There was now nothing for it, but to drive into Clevedon and trawl through the electoral roll at the town's Crown Post Office, right opposite the Mercury in Six Ways.

The journey should have taken me 20 minutes at the most, but I encountered heavy traffic and had difficulty finding somewhere to park, so it was over half an hour before I was able to study the electoral roll.

Alas there was no sign of him living in the Walton ward, but 'bingo' I spotted him in a neighbouring one and five minutes later I was outside his bungalow in a quiet and leafy road.

Nobody came to the door despite several loud knocks. Now I must say at this point, that the question of success or failure had simply not entered my head, because I was totally focussed on achieving my objective and the adrenalin was flowing.

A peep through his low-level letterbox revealed quite a pile of mail on the mat, so he was obviously away, but just as I was walking away and pondering on what to do next, a car dove slowly passed and turned into the drive opposite, and I was there in a flash.

They were an elderly couple, who had just returned from shopping and happily confirmed that their neighbours had gone off on holiday a couple of days earlier. "Do you know where?" I asked.

"Oh, yes, because we feed their cats and have an emergency number for them, but why do you want to know?" the woman asked guardedly'

When I produced my Press card and explained the reason for my enquiry, they told me that Mr Reynolds and his wife were staying in an hotel in the South Devon seaside town of Paignton.

I waited outside their open front door while they went inside and found the number, which I hurriedly scribbled into my notebook.

I had spotted a red telephone box on a corner a couple of hundred yards away and was soon on the phone to the hotel receptionist, who put me through to their room with the remark that she was not sure they would still be in at this time of the morning.

I waited with the proverbial bated breath and a moment later Mr Reynolds answered.

He was highly amused when I explained the reason for the call and all the effort, I had gone to track him down and happily confirmed the positive news story that my colleague back in the office had been struggling to stand up.

"You were extremely lucky to catch us in, because if my wife had not a disturbed night, we would certainly have left by now," was his parting shot.

That was the fascinating thing about being a reporter, because one never knew just what was going to happen next.

But that being the case, there was one continuing story to which I would return time after time again from my joining the Post in January 1970, right through until the end of the decade, and that was the fight to save Clevedon Pier.

Over the years its marooned pier head had rusted into a sorry state, but it had become a safe roost for tens of thousands of starlings, whose mass murmurations were a delight to watch.

While the Pier Supporters Club was formed in embryo by those standing around in the car park after that Clevedon Urban District Council meeting, I had attended on the day the pier fell down, a Pier Preservation Trust was also founded.

Members later set up a Technical Group, including those with professional knowledge. to come up with realistic proposals and costings for the replacing of the two missing spans.

But despite all their best efforts, the successor Woodspring District Council, which took over in 1974, decided not to invest ratepayers' cash in a restoration project, but instead obtained a Court Order to pull the whole structure down.

I was not at that fateful meeting because it was held in Weston-super-Mare, but I picked up immediately on the tidal wave of anger and consternation that swept across Clevedon in the aftermath.

And I was certainly there to cover the public inquiry, held the following March at Clevedon's Sunhill Park Community Centre, where my mum and I had fallen asleep in the middle of those three one act plays.

Pier Supporters Club members, including the indefatigable farmer's wife, Hilda Baker, arrived in period Victorian costume, which was a gift of a photo opportunity, and Paul Chadd, QC, the Bristol barrister engaged by the Trust, presented a large number of depositions, received in favour of saving the historic structure.

A capacity audience listened intently to a recorded message from the Poet Laureate, Sir John Betjeman, who spoke of Clevedon's pier being the most beautiful in England and that its loss would be a tragedy - Clevedon without its pier, would be like a diamond with a flaw, he said.

Then the inquiry heard detailed and extensive evidence, gathered by the Trust's Technical Group, including realistic costings, which showed how the pier could be restored.

That, in my opinion, was the weight which finally tipped the judgement in favour of saving the pier.

After that momentous decision, if my memory serves me right, Woodspring Council handed the pier over to the Trust, which was reformed from the Technical Group, and a whole wave of stories ensued as grant applications were made to such august bodes as the Historic Buildings Council.

Over 40 years have now floated past since I attended that inquiry and I now retain only three crystal clear memories of the proceedings, the first being those supporters in their Victorian costumes, the second hearing Sir John Betjeman's resonant voice and the third being a response to some argument made by the council's side.

"That, ladies and gentlemen, is the biggest red herring that never swam up the Bristol Channel!"

BECOMING A SHIPPING CORRESPONDENT

Because I worked out in North Somerset, I was usually among the last to hear the office gossip or of any internal changes, so when I found out, quite by chance, that the Shipping Correspondent's job was up for grabs, I assumed the position had already been filled.

I clearly remember driving across the sunlit moors from Clevedon Court towards the village of Yatton, when it suddenly struck me that I wanted that particular reporting job and I wanted it above all else!

But just what had prompted this entirely new ambition? I did not give that a thought at the time, but later in a more reflective moment, I easily worked it out.

When I was aged six, we moved down from Bristol to an apartment overlooking Clevedon Pier, and I would often stand in the garden watching the cargo ships sailing away down channel and over the horizon and into the big wide world beyond.

This had left an indelible impression on me, as had the word "Avonmouth," from whence those ships had come.

"Yes choo, choo, choo all the way to Avonmouth," my grandmother, Nanny Heath, would often say as I trotted along the metal grill of a storm drain near her house in Westbury-upon Trym, pretending to be a train.

Back in those days, my father, John, headed up the Accident Investigation Department at the now long-gone Atlas Insurance Company in Bristol City Centre and would occasionally come home and tell Mum that he had been out to the scene of some industrial accident at Avonmouth.

And then, when my beloved Auntie Lil looked after me, we often sat at the table in her little flat in Waverley Road, Redland, making clothes-peg boats, so it was easy to see why the prospect of being the paper's shipping writer had suddenly and unexpectedly excited me.

When I got back home to Congresbury, I immediately called up the then News Editor, Jeremy Brien. No, the job was still open, but it was a Head Office post, he pointed out.

Now I really wanted the job, but there was no way I was ever going to give up my free and easy roving life to go and work in Bristol!

"Look, Bristol's controversial new and loss-making Royal Portbury Dock is actually on my patch and from there, I can be over the Avon Bridge and into Avonmouth in ten minutes," I pointed out.

When I told Jeremy I was confident that I could easily combine my district reporter's job covering North Somerset with looking after the port, he said he would see what our editor, Gordon Farnsworth, had to say,

I became the Post's Shipping Correspondent on a Friday afternoon on the understanding that it was for a trial period only, and on the following Monday morning, the port was suddenly plunged into one of the longest pay disputes in its maritime history.

It was indeed a baptism of fire, but by the time industrial peace had finally been restored some six weeks later, I had made the job exclusively my own.

The City Council-owned port had become a heavy loss maker with 29p in every pound of ratepayers' cash going to support it, so its affairs were always of great interest to the Evening Post and rate paying readers.

Port trade had made a huge contribution to Bristol's economic prosperity for hundreds of years and when sail gave way to steam and wooden hulls to those of iron and steel, the city docks, linked to the coast and the outside world by the meandering tidal River Avon, became too small, so a new complex was developed at Avonmouth.

The port, now able to receive vessels of up to 30,000 tonnes at its Royal Edward Docks, went on growing and flourishing up until the 1950s and early 1960s, with ships literally queuing up to enter with cargoes of meat and butter from Australia and New Zealand, tea from India, fruit from the West Indies and oils, grains, animal feeds and general goods from around the world.

Bristol had always benefited because it was the UK's Western gateway to the Atlantic, but as ships grew even larger, the city fathers began to realize that the port would eventually lose out to rivals such as Southampton and Liverpool, if it was unable to receive the latest generation vessels.

The answer, they perceived, was to build a huge new dock with the biggest sea locks in the UK, on the other side of the river at Portbury, but there was a problem because the government of the day declined to subsidise the £40 million cost.

City councillors were in a dilemma because to go it alone would be a huge and costly undertaking, yet without that facility, the port and the many thousands of jobs depending on it would inevitably decline.

They decided to go ahead with the project anyway and the Royal Portbury Dock was eventually opened by the Queen in 1977, but by this time the tide of commercial fortunes had already begun turning against Bristol.

The UK's entry into the Common Market, signalled the end of the Australian and New Zealand butter and meat trades and with Britain, now effectively turning its back on its Commonwealth partners and looking to Europe, Bristol was suddenly on the wrong side of the country.

To make matters worse, the new generation container shipping companies calling in Europe and the UK, found it more cost-effective to discharge their boxes in Southampton or Felixstowe, before going on to the Continent rather than diverting up the Bristol Channel to Bristol.

By the time I took over as Shipping Correspondent, all the chickens had started coming home to roost.

Some of the ship working arrangement concessions made to the labour force in time of plenty when large profits were being made year-on-year, started proving restrictive in the struggle to cut costs and remain competitive.

This coupled with the crippling interest repayments on the new dock, meant that the port was now losing around £10 million a year.

Once the port pay dispute had been settled and I came up for air, I suggested to the Editor that I should write "A Day in the Life Of" feature on key people in the docks industry.

He agreed and the City Council-controlled Port of Bristol Authority was happy to assist, so I was able to use this strategy to start learning as much as I could about the docks industry.

I first accompanied a Bristol Channel pilot as he brought a big ship safely in from the sea and this entailed a most memorable, if not a little scary day out.

We were taken by car to Barry, where I was fitted with a buoyancy aid and we boarded a sturdy pilot cutter and sped over the waves out to rendezvous with a bulk cargo ship, now making her way slowly up channel towards Avonmouth.

Hanging tightly onto a guard rail, and balancing to stay upright, I watched as we came up behind the towering vessel and started coming along the port side with the pilot boat skipper using his powerful engines to prevent the swell tossing us onto the side of the hull.

Now, just ahead, I spotted an open door in the side of the ship from which a sturdy rope ladder with flat wooden rungs, dangled, and up which I would soon be having to climb!

The channel pilot, who had completed this manoeuvre in all winds and weathers many times before, chose his moment and stepping nimbly onto the ladder, swifty climbed the short distance to the door and was helped inside by two crew members standing on either side of the opening.

Oh, my God, now it was my turn!

With a roar of its powerful twin engines, the cutter moved away from the hull for few brief seconds, before coming alongside and with a helping hand from a crew member, I too stepped onto the facing ladder and made the brief climb to be grabbed and helped inside by two strong pairs of arms.

Within minutes, we had been escorted up to the bridge, high above the waves, where an air of calm prevailed as the helmsman kept us on course, while the captain, mug of coffee in hand, turned to greet us and ordered his ship to resume her former speed.

It was always 'pilot's advice to master's orders,' the pilot had explained on the ride out from Avonmouth, and having shaken hands with the master, he stepped forward and peering ahead, began issuing instructions to the helmsman.

"Port ten" and a little later "starboard fifteen" etc, as he guided the ship up the marked channel.

The time seemed to pass very quickly while I stood in the background, watching and taking in the whole fascinating process, as we slowly approached the wide open Avonmouth lock gates.

The weather and state of the sea was reasonably calm on this most memorable occasion.

But as we passed the new Royal Portbury Dock, which could receive vessels of up to 100,000 tonnes, I fully appreciated the skill of the channel pilots having to manoeuvre giant container and bulk cargo ships safely into port in high winds, when their sheer sides of steel could also act as sails!

Climbing into a crane driver's lonely cab, high above the quay, was also a great experience, but after that, I kept my feet firmly on the ground, spending a day with port's tight knit team of British Transport Docks Police and, even more fascinatingly, with the Customs squad and hearing many amazing tales of foiled drug smuggling attempts.

The Customs Officers got to know which ships sailing in from South and Central America and from the India and African continents were possible drug smuggling contenders and would organise random searches by the Rummage Squad, who would go aboard and search all the by-now-customary hiding places.

By the time I had completed my interview and a Post photographer had nipped down from Bristol to take my suggested pictures, I too came away with my own precious cargo, namely the personal contact details of many of my interviewees, with whom by now I was on Christian name terms

While my predecessor shipping reporters had, to some extent, been chained to head office by virtue of being based there, I on the other hand, was completely free to come and go as I pleased.

Once I had fulfilled my morning obligations by supplying two or three reasonable stories from my patch and had sent over a couple of pieces for the following day, there was nothing to stop me spending the rest of my time in the docks.

I quickly discovered that the Avonmouth shipping agencies played a key role in the life of the port industry.

They were the middle men, who represented the shipping lines and liaised with Captains and the Port Authority over ship working times.

Once a ship had docked, they were her Master's representative and provided him with all manner of port related services.

I started making calls on all the agents and within six months I had infiltrated virtually every area of port life with the result that if there was some new traffic on the horizon, or a shipping company was sailing away, then it was not long before I knew about it.

I was therefore able to be first with the news that: "Port Wins New Trade" or "Port Set to Lose Trade" stories, and, also to open the can on issues, which either the Port Authority or the unions would rather I had not uncovered.

I know I was often a thorn in the side of one party or the other and that my activities did not always make life easy for the members of the port's always professional and helpful Press and Publicity department, who were continually having to field my calls and enquiries.

I made them particularly annoyed on one memorable occasion when the guided missile destroyer, HMS Bristol, was paying a courtesy visit to her adopted home city.

I went onboard and suddenly noticed that the Type 42 guided missile destroyer had been moored up right opposite a Russian freighter with the Hammer and Sickle clearly visible on its funnel.

I had a photographer with me at the time and simply could not resist setting up a picture showing some unsuspecting naval officer with the Russian flag appearing over his shoulder.

My story suggested that perhaps the unfortunate positioning of these two vessels was not exactly in the best interests of UK security.

Looking back now, I feel this had been pretty mischievous on my part and I apologise to all those affected by the fall-out from this particular story.

Anyway, the port's Press Officers soon forgave me for my HMS Bristol and hammer and sickle story and a few weeks later I was invited by the Royal Navy to go aboard the destroyer in Portsmouth - not to walk the plank, but to report on a three-naval exercise out in the English Channel

And I was not the first one to sometimes give the port authority a hard time.

There is a wonderful, and I don't believe apocryphal story of the day that the harassed port press officer was called in by irate port bosses to be shown an Evening Post aerial picture of a completely empty Royal Portbury Dock.

"What are we going to do about this?" they demanded. "Well, we don't have any anti-aircraft guns," came the dry reply.

I soon became aware that all the port agents received their daily copy of the broadsheet, Lloyds List, based in Colchester, Essex, which was the international bible of the global ports industry and contained daily lists of world-wide shipping movements.

The paper also carried news stories from ports around the UK and overseas, so not many weeks went by before I called their News Editor and offered to send in news pieces from the Port of Bristol.

My offer was gladly accepted and it was not many more weeks before a series of always positive stories by Nigel Heath started raising the council-owned port's profile and for which I started receiving regular payments, certainly an added incentive.

Of course, all the bad news stories, and there were quite a few of those, were kept exclusively for the Post and its increasingly-exasperated reader ratepayers, who were footing port losses to the tune of £10 million a year.

The plain fact of the matter was that if I sent negative stories to Lloyds for all the world to see, then doors would very quickly start closing around me and, apart from that, I certainly did not want to be disloyal to the many people who were being extremely helpful to me and relied on the port for their livelihoods.

Bristol, like the majority of its rivals, was a National Dock Labour Scheme port, where registered dockers were virtually guaranteed a job for life and whose work was the subject of a number of restrictive practices built over the years.

But the problem was that the concessions so easily made to port workers in the 1940s and 1950s when cargo ships carrying meat imports from Australia and New Zealand and tens of thousands of chests of tea from India, were lining up to enter Avonmouth, were proving costly, once leaner times came over the horizon in the 1960s and 1970s.

The port was manned by over 1,000 dockers, who operated under a system whereby, as I recall, they would receive a quarter night's extra pay if cargo handling went on after 5pm, a half night if they worked to finish a ship after 7pm and a whole night's extra pay and the next day off if cargo handling went on beyond 9pm.

I can't remember the number of times a frustrated port agent would tip me off with the news that the very last piece of cargo had been landed just a few minutes after 7pm.

The heydays had well and truly ended by the time I started covering the port in the early 1970s, yet it still had a large dock side railway labour force and two independent tug companies the local operator, CJ King, and the South Wales-based, Cory Ship Towage.

Our in-house rival, the WDP, had a succession of port reporters, who like me, attended the monthly Docks Committee meetings, in the Port of Bristol Authority's HQ and several, I quickly realised and, accepted, were better journalists than me.

But they simply could not compete with all the news gathering time I was spending in and around the dock estate.

Based at Avonmouth in those days was the Royal Mail ship, RMS St Helena, which sailed from the port every seven weeks on a round trip voyage to the remote British islands of Ascension and St Helena and then on down to Cape Town, South Africa.

Whereas Ascension had an air base, St Helena was a tiny volcanic speck far out in the South Atlantic, so before an air strip was built in more recent times, the ship was the islanders' only link with the outside world.

The supply vessel carried absolutely everything needed to sustain life for the 5,000, then fiercely-loyal British subjects, on this far-flung outpost of the old British Empire, so on any single voyage the St Helena could be carrying anything from livestock to nappies and from beer to high explosives, which meant there was always something interesting to write about.

We had just finished supper one evening when one of my port contacts telephoned to tell me that the ship had just made an unscheduled call at Lundy Island in the Bristol Channel, to pick up some visitors, who had been left stranded for several days because it had been too rough for the island's small supply boat to pick them up.

So, I called up photographer, Bob Bowen, who was a near neighbour, and we met up at the entrance to Avonmouth Docks an hour later.

I signalled for him to follow, as I headed out to the lock gates, because if we could catch the ship in the locks, we could board her there and would have at least twenty minutes to take our pictures and do some interviews before she berthed in the Royal Edward Dock.

Bob's Image: Ian Newton

My plan worked a treat and Bob and I were just completing our task, when we were unceremoniously hauled up before the captain and a very annoyed customs officer.

"What do you think you were doing boarding this ship, while she was still technically inward bound?" he demanded.

"I could throw the book at you, you know. We have more power than the police and I could detain you both," he told us.

We protested our ignorance and apologised profusely and he eventually calmed down and let us go.

But it was not the end of that most memorable evening for Bob, because he then had to drive in to Bristol to drop off his film at the Evening Post office.

The good old, RMS St Helena, was to come up trumps yet again as a great source of news stories and this time in spectacular fashion on the day that Prince Charles married Diana in July 1981

Looking for a Page One lead local angle on a royal wedding day, when there really is only one main story, is always a headache for regional newspaper editors.

I just happened to be making one of my customary courtesy calls to the ship, a couple of days earlier when someone happened to remark that it was a pity that the St Helena islanders would be missing out on all the celebrations, especially when they were so fiercely patriotic with a Union Jack in almost every home.

The island was still one of the few populated places in the world where television had yet to arrive.

There ensued a general discussion on the subject, out of which came the idea that if we put a large screen television on the ship with a VHS recorder, then the islanders would at least be able to watch the wedding on a video as soon as the ship arrived.

However, there were two small drawbacks to this plan, the first being that we had to acquire the costly equipment, and second and far more importantly, the ship was due to sail from Avonmouth before the wedding had taken place and therefore before the video could be recorded.

Luckily, one of my contacts in nearby Portishead, was television shop proprietor, Cliff Freeman, who willingly agreed to loan the islanders a large screen TV, together with a video recorder, which I helped him carry on board.

It also transpired, that one of the ship's engineering cadets, Myron Benjamin, who had been studying in the UK, was due to fly out to rejoin the ship when she arrived at Tenerife.

So this meant that he was able to carry the video recording of the wedding that took place while the RMS St Helena was en route from Avonmouth.

The Evening Post's seven-column wide Page One headline on Charles and Di's wedding day said it all, although with a bit of journalistic licence.

> **EVENING POST**
>
> SHIPSHAPE AND BRISTOL TV FASHION
>
> # The Post man speeds Wedding film
>
> It goes to lonely St Helena
>
> By Nigel Heath
>
> It's 5p more on gallon of petrol
>
> Royal London bursts at the seams
>
> CITY IS HIT BY NIGHT RIOTS AGAIN
>
> ANNA IS GOING TO HAVE A BABY

The enterprising Mr Freeman was shown alongside my picture byline, presenting the set to the captain.

He went on to supply televisions and video equipment to the St Helena islanders for years to come. They could not receive television, but they could watch videos!

Another great story of enterprise came when I received a tip off that the Yeovil, Somerset- based, Abbey Hill Group, was poised to open a major car import centre on the Royal Portbury Dock estate and that sent me in search of its Chairman and Managing Director, Roger Bastable.

Roger had originally gained a degree in economics and had worked with Leyland Management for a year, but in his spare time, he, and several friends, would drive together to car auctions, return with three or four cars, and sell then on the forecourt of local pubs, in an around Yeovil.

He had told me: "This little enterprise proved so successful, that it occurred to me that if we acquired a couple of old car transporters, we could scale up the operation.

"So, I borrowed £14,000 and launched my second-hand car dealership on a five-acre lot at Abbey Hill in the town."
Roger painted his transporters bright yellow with the words, Abbey Hill Group Yeovil, and his telephone number, painted in orange on the side.

Then he was in his Portacabin office one afternoon, when he received an out of the blue call from a Datsun transport manager, who had noticed one of his transporters parked up in Brighton - actually, it had broken down.

"This manager told me he had not realised there was a car transporter company operating in the West Country and would I be able to handle the import of 40,000 Datsuns through Poole Harbour," Roger explained.

"I asked him – 'When would you need them, because mine are all out on a Post Office contract, at the moment?', having just spotted a telecoms engineer working on a pole outside my window"

Roger went into overdrive, managed to put together a fleet of 11 transporters, handled the contract and went on to build up a considerable South of England operation handling thousands of cars for a number of importers.

Every year, Lloyds List, carried a major feature on the Port of Bristol and it was customary for the local port reporter to write it.

The paper required 6,000 words, a mighty number when compared to my every day news stories, which hardly ever exceeded twelve short paragraphs,

Still, Lloyds was paying £800 for 6,000 words, a considerable sum at the time, so I had no hesitation in accepting this windfall commission.

The feature gave me the opportunity of consolidating all that I had learnt about the port industry over the past eight months and to write at greater depths about individual trades and companies.

I was now working an almost flat-out 14-hour day, making my first call to the news desk around 7.45am, writing North Somerset copy until around 3.45pm and then starting work on the feature after a short rest, a play with our children, Robin and Natalie, if they were not watching Chock-A-Block, and having some tea.

At last, after a four weeks slog, the task was finally completed and I called Bob Jordan, the Lloyds' Features Editor, a couple of days later to make sure my precious parcel, including pictures, willingly supplied by the port authority, had arrived safely.

It was a moment in time that I shall never forget. It was late afternoon and I was sitting at my desk in a sunny room, which doubled as my study and a second family sitting room.

"Yes, I have the feature," Bob confirmed, and then, suddenly as if from nowhere, I heard myself asking: "I don't suppose you have any others you want doing?"

There was a pause - "How about Antwerp? he replied. I heard myself readily agreeing and I came off the phone with instructions to call, Anita Sparrow, the paper's travel organiser to make my flight and hotel arrangements, for which Lloyds would pay.

"What have you just done?" I said aloud, staring almost in disbelief at the telephone with rising feelings of both doubt and excitement.

'Lloyds require 10,000 words for Antwerp, so that will be loads more dosh,' said my Mr Positive.

'Yes, but Antwerp is Europe's second busiest port and you know absolutely nothing about it, so surely you have bitten off far more than you can chew,' Mr Negative responded.

I then had a funny, and by now vaguely familiar feeling, which has returned to me at certain times in my life, when I am full of doubts, but I know deep down that I am going to do it anyway.

I easily arranged to take a week of my precious four weeks holiday and then put in a call to the Port of Antwerp Marketing and Publicity Department.

Copyright: Port of Antwerp

From then on in was pretty much plain sailing because they in turn arranged a whole series of interviews for me with key port cargo handling companies and Lloyds sent me copies of the Antwerp feature from the previous two years. so that I could read up on the port in advance.

I caught an evening flight from Heathrow to Antwerp, took a cab to an excellent city centre hotel, already pre-booked by Lloyds, and duly presented myself at the magnificent centuries-old city hall at 9am the following morning.

I spent my first day with a port authority publicity executive, who gave me an extensive tour of the vast docks complex, a launch cruise along the port gateway, River Scheldt, and enough background notes to fill both sides of one of my tape recorder cassettes.

Day two promised to be far more demanding because I was to interview the chairman of one of Antwerp's main cargo handling terminals, followed by other top people in the port industry.

Such was the prestige which Lloyds commanded that they had all made time to see me and I was sure they were not going to suffer fools gladly!

Luckily, articles had been written about all of them in the earlier features, so I spent the evening in the hotel reading and re-reading them and making lists of questions which, I hoped, would help me to avoid showing my general lack of knowledge.

It was all a far cry from that afternoon, only eight month earlier, when I walked into my first shipping agency office in Avonmouth and naively asked its boss: "What do you do?"

Heart beating slightly faster than normal, I followed a personal secretary into a large and wood-panelled Antwerp inner sanctum to meet my first interviewee, who stepped out from behind his enormous desk to greet me.

He ushered me to one of two leather arm chairs beside an ornate coffee table and when we were both seated, smiled and asked: "And what do you think of your Iron Lady?"

I was completely thrown off course by the sudden question, but from the way he asked it, I guessed he was a fan of Margaret Thatcher.

Luckily, I was right and we spent an interesting five minutes discussing the merits of Britain's first woman Prime Minister before getting down to talking about his giant container handling terminal and how he saw its future progressing.

All went well at that interview and with those which followed during the rest of the week with the Iron Lady mostly being the first topic of conversation.

I returned home with nine cassette tapes, each containing 90 minutes of interviews to type out as part of writing the Antwerp epic, and all in my own time, so I was going to be working late into the evening for weeks.

This was to set the pattern for years to come, with a week of my precious family holidays being spent jetting off at Lloyds' expense to write features on ports including the Northern Netherlands, Amsterdam, Ravenna, in Italy, where embarrassingly, no one had been told I was coming, the Canary Islands and the Channel Islands.

I also wrote about Southampton, to the annoyance of a fellow journo on the local Evening Echo, a commission I would have declined, had I known he was there, the Cornish English China Clay ports of Fowey and Par and also the East Coast ports of Hull and Kings Lynn.

I found out which UK ports were not already being covered by Lloyds' correspondents and began reporting on shipping affairs in Newhaven, Shoreham, Exmouth, Teignmouth, Kings Lynn and others.

I also made time to write to more than 50 major ports around the world, requesting their annual reports and press releases, which I then turned into stories for Lloyds and other shipping publications.

I soon got to know all about the bulk coal terminals in Queensland, Australia, container and car handling in the Port of Halifax, Nova Scotia, and the cargoes passing through the Port of Auckland, New Zealand.

I even negotiated with a shipping newspaper in Australia to write a regular column on shipping in the UK, but that never went ahead.

I had been reporting on shipping news from Halifax, Nova Scotia, for a couple of years, when, right out of the blue, I got the chance to go there officially and on behalf of the Evening Post.

It all came about because I had previously written a feature on the part-time sailors of the Royal Naval Reserve, whose own minesweeper, HMS Caron, was based in the city docks.

I got to hear that a Bristol crew was to sail the ship across the North Atlantic to take part in a historic Canadian naval review and that a second relief party would then fly out from Brize Norton, Oxfordshire, courtesy of the RAF, to bring the vessel home again.

A BBC regional reporter and film crew were also flying out with the relief crew to cover the event and would be coming home a week later with Air Canada and I was invited to accompany them.

Great, I thought, I get to make my first trip to Canada to write about HMS Caron and her crew and I will also have the opportunity of calling on the port authority and making some good contacts. But unfortunately, it did not work out quite as planned.

A coach picked us all up from HMS Caron's shore base in Bristol and drove us to RAF Brize Norton in Oxfordshire. where we boarded an RAF passenger jet, only to find that all the seats were facing backwards, clearly a safer option.

Meanwhile, across the pond in Montreal, a suitcase containing a bomb, believed to have been planted by Sikh extremists, was being loaded into the baggage hold of Air India flight 182, bound for Europe.

It exploded off the coast of Ireland on June 23, 1985, with the loss of all 329 Passengers and crew.

Blissfully unaware of all this, I was fast asleep in a basic motel bedroom close to the port, when the bedside phone rang in my ear and I was instantly awake and grabbing the phone to hear Post News Editor Jeremy Brien's voice.

The clock on my bedside radio alarm told me that it was 4am in Halifax, but it was 8am in the UK and having briefed me on the disaster, Jeremy asked me if I could file a piece from the Canadian angle by 11am UK time.

Staggering out of bed, I made a mug of coffee and switched on CNN to watch the story unfolding before my tired eyes.

Retrieving my notebook from my case, which had yet to be unpacked, I began making notes and found it surprisingly easy to put something together and phone it over for the 11am deadline, after which I went in search of some breakfast.

It might have been flaming June in Bristol, but it was damp, overcast and misty in Halifax, which rather set the tone, as I continued phoning over a couple of stories a day for the next three days.

I managed an afternoon visit to the nearby picturesque Peggy's Cove with its houses perched above a narrow inlet, a safe haven for fishing boats, but again the weather was dull and I did not think it was a patch on Cornwall.

I later enjoyed being taken around the container port by its enthusiastic commercial manager, who promised me a regular supply of their port newsletters and was as good as his word.

The naval review was staged towards the end of the week and I went aboard HMS Caron and carried out some interviews for the feature I would write after my Air Canada overnight flight home.

While all my ports and shipping work was going on, I also went to great lengths to ensure that my regular district reporting job did not suffer.

All my years of covering North Somerset, meant that I had it pretty much sewn up with reliable contacts in every town and village and thanks also to my follow-up diary system, I was able to continue giving the news desk a steady flow of copy.

I was now making quite a considerable sum from my freelance shipping activities and the more I earned, the more I wanted.

It was as if I had become hooked on the excitement of finding the shipping stories. followed by the gratification of turning them into cash.

But inevitably there was a price to pay in lost time with my precious family and a gradual draining of my inner resources.

It all came to a climax as I sat in a taxi in a traffic jam on a scorching Monday morning in the centre of Santa Cruz de Tenerife and on my official holidays.

'What the hell are you doing here?' I asked myself. 'This is crazy. You simply can't go on like this any more!'

When I got home, with another dozen tape-recorded interviews to plough through, Clevedon Flower Show had come around again for the 20th time.

I surprised myself by feeling really depressed as I wandered around the large show tent on The Salthouse Field on a Friday afternoon, trying to rake up some enthusiasm.

It was no good - I had to face it. I had lost all interest in local events, which I had now been covering since my junior reporter days, and simply could not go on living this double life any longer, because for one thing my health was going to suffer!

So, what was to be done about it? I asked myself and by and by, a possible answer came to me.

I had now established my reputation as an international shipping correspondent and had generated a considerable amount of positive publicity for my home Port of Bristol, so might the port authority now be prepared to retain my shipping PR services?

I knew Doug Naysmith, then, port chairman, pretty-well by this time, so I laid out my thoughts over a lunch-time pint in a small pub close to the city council offices on College Green and he was receptive to the idea and promised to see what he could do to take my proposal further.

Doug went on to become the much-respected Labour MP for Bristol North West from 1997, until standing down at the 2010 General Election and our paths later crossed again because of his interest in the campaign to return the Bristol-based day trip passenger ship, MV Balmoral, to cruising in the Bristol Channel.

I was much saddened to hear of his passing at the time of writing this book.

Anyway, to return to my story, I was lucky that the Port Director could also see the advantages of having me 'come aboard' and I was given a year's contract to spend eight days a month actively promoting the port.

The agreed fee, plus my existing earnings from shipping journalism, more than covered my Evening Post salary, so suddenly the door to a new life, no longer pressured by daily deadlines, and freed forever from parish pump, magically swung open.

However, I was giving up a seemingly-secure job with a car and a telephone to live on my wits and by my own endeavours and some senior members of my family thought I was a fool.

"Don't do it, Daddy, because we'll starve," implored my nine-year-old, Natalie, as we walked down to the village newsagents the following Sunday morning.

She had clearly been ear-wigging on a conversation, I had had with my then father-in-law, but there was no going back now.

It was a bright Wednesday afternoon in 1989 when I walked into Editor Brian Jones' office to hand in my resignation before going out to break the news to my head office colleagues.

Some looked at me in disbelief, because after 17 years I had become something of a fixture, but when I walked out of the staff exit of the Temple Way building on that never-to-be-forgotten afternoon and suddenly turned and looked back, I felt a huge weight lifting from my shoulders.

In true nautical fashion, my leaving party was a cruise on the paddle steamer, Waverley, from the city docks to Clevedon Pier, with editor Brian Jones shaking my hand as my colleagues looked on.

Editor Brian Jones bids me farewell

And, as if specially ordered by some divine hand, the very last piece I wrote for the paper was a hot-off-the-press shipping story!

The Bristol sand dredger, Harry Brown, and the sewage disposal boat, Glen Avon, managed to collide almost head-on in the sea entrance to the River Avon, early on my final morning with the paper.

Just after leaving the Post, I had negotiated a £350 per month fee to promote a new shipping service from an East Coast port to the Continent, but this foundered before its maiden voyage and before I had received my first fee.

Suddenly I felt vulnerable and very much aware that I had entered a whole new world of uncertainties.

The following morning, I received a call from the Port Director, who asked me to prepare a schedule of the shipping conferences regularly held in major port venues around the world, so that the port authority could consider taking a stand or sending a representative.

I knew that Lloyds List staged some conferences, so I asked them for their dates and a very helpful girl in the promotions department gave me the contact details of another conference and events company, called World Trade Promotions.

My call to them rang out on an empty desk in an office somewhere in Surrey and was answered by the managing director who happened to be passing by.

"Are you a shipping expert?" he asked after, I had explained what I wanted.

"Yes," I replied, without a moment's hesitation. "Well maybe you could help us by supplying lists of companies, who might take stands at our forthcoming exhibitions," he suggested.

We met two days later and the company agreed to pay me £350 a month for the listings, which I could easily source from those taking advertising space in trade publications. and from all the literature which was now flowing in from ports all around the world.

The following week, I took my young family to stay in a comfortable vegetarian B&B, near Ashburton in Devon, and made day trips to Dartmeet and other beauty spots around Dartmoor.

The sun shone every day, we were all having fun, and in the evenings, we ate at a little bistro in the town.

I had the most wonderful feeling of being, really free, for the first time in many years; free from daily deadlines and free to decide my own destiny from here on in.

MY PR YEARS

I had moved my office to the spare bedroom in my widowed Mum's house in Congresbury several years earlier, in order to separate home and work, and was thinking of winding up for the day, when a telephone call came that was to change my life and fortunes for many years to come.

Six months prior to leaving the Post and launching my own sole trader enterprise, which I called, Media-Consult, I had also started covering the Bristol Airport management committee meetings, another responsibility from which, I was able to walk away.

But they still had my contact details, so when a call came in from a tour operator complaining about an alleged inaccurate story, which had appeared in the Western Daily Press, they passed the caller on to me.

When the caller had finished her explanation, I told her that I had never heard of Aspro Holidays, so could she very kindly enlighten me?

Aspro, it transpired, was a family-run Cardiff-based tour operator, which sold package holidays to their home island of Cyprus and also to Spain, Portugal and Greece.

They used their own airline, Inter European Airways, which operated flights from Cardiff, Bristol and Belfast, carrying around 60,000 holiday makers every year.

"So, who handles your press and publicity?" I asked. "Well, no one," came the surprising and totally unexpected reply.

About a month later, following a series of, back and forth, phone calls, I was invited over to Aspro House, an imposing pillar-fronted building in Bute Street, Cardiff, a relic from the Welsh capital's once illustrious maritime past.

On stepping inside on that momentous summer morning in 1989, I found myself in what I can only describe as a package holiday-making factory.

The whole place was literally buzzing with activity, as dozens of staff in numerous departments from telesales to brochure production, overseas operations, and cabin services, were all busily beavering away under one roof to keep pace with what was the peak holiday season for this burgeoning travel business.

There was a visual and audible vibrancy to all that was happening inside Aspro House, which reminded me vividly of the Evening Post's old Silver Street news room with its busy, busy reporters, telephones jammed to their ears, and the constant clatter of chattering typewriters.

All a far cry from today's often impersonal and soulless open plan newsrooms where figures sit as if transfixed in front of glowing computer screens.

The tangible buzz at Aspro House greatly excited me and I just knew it was going to be an ever-flowing source of some great news stories.

It was agreed the company would initially pay me £500 per month to produce a steady supply of news publicity in Cardiff, Bristol, and Belfast and to handle all future media issues and enquiries.

This was to be my three-month trial and honeymoon period with Aspro and I was determined to shower them with news coverage cuttings like they were confetti!

I was given a conducted tour of the building and introduced to all the key heads of department on whom I could call for information on all aspects of the business.

Aspro sold its holidays through travel agents, who were not already tied to one of the big-league tour operators and were therefore more independent.

Not a bad morning's work, I mused as I began driving home and mentally totted up my new total income.

I would now be earning over £2,500 a month without having to work half as hard as I did in newspapers.

But although I had no way of knowing it at the time, I had just caught a holiday industry tiger cub by its tail.

Taking good care of its network of independent agents was an important part of the Aspro marketing strategy and, in the course of doing so, the company had unknowingly created a particularly brilliant news PR opportunity.

The agents and their sales teams, whose clients mainly flew from Bristol for example, would be invited to the airport for a reception.

But what they did not know was that they were to be whisked off for a dinner in the sky, which of course, made a great story and picture opportunity for all their local papers.

Former Evening Post Picture Editor Terry Dite and I met at the airport on a glorious late summer evening to launch our first major Aspro PR exercise.

The boys and girls from holiday shops for miles around, began arriving, often straight from a manic day's selling, and were ready to relax and have some fun.

Working feverishly from a guest list, I quickly identified key groups of agents for Terry to picture as they boarded the IEA jet conveniently parked close by.

The plan was to have a picture of a holiday shop team from as many different newspaper circulation areas as possible so that every story would be "local" to them and would therefore have the best chance of being used.

The tricky bit was to act quickly, so as not hold up the boarding operation and in turn, the flight.

Having rapidly circulated the steadily expanding and by now noisy drinks party, we finally managed to prise our little groups away from their friends and colleagues and shepherd them outside and on to the tarmac to be pictured with the Inter European logoed 737.

It was all good fun, but I can see airport security men having collective heart attacks if anyone tried to repeat this sort of stunt in these sad days of global terror.

Ever the true professional, Terry easily got some great pictures, but I was left fumbling with my notebook and pencil trying to get all the names in the right order and at speed, while our other groups champed restlessly at the bit waiting for their turn.

It was like being confronted by that growing army of impatient mourners outside St Andrews Church in Clevedon, all over again.

But we got the job done and soon our IEA 737 was jetting up, up and away with its merry band of travel agents and Terry and me riding PR shotgun with my notebook and his camera.

The result was a great success with virtually every local paper carrying the "Surprise Dinner in the Sky" story and picture and, of course, the all-important message about flying off on holiday from your own local Airport with Aspro and Inter European.

We naturally repeated this brilliant exercise at Cardiff Airport and later at East Midlands, where for once things did not go quite according to plan.

There had been a suggestion that Terry and I would fly up with the aircraft from Cardiff, but we had decided in the end to drive, simply because we would not have had any time to organise our all-important pictures had we flown.

It was another lovely sunny evening and the travel agents' reception was in full and noisy swing in a lounge with wide views over the runway, but there was only one thing missing from the scene and that was our flying restaurant.

I got that horrible sinking feeling in the pit of my stomach and called up IEA operations in Cardiff on my newly and proudly acquired brick-size mobile to find out where it was.

"Oh, it's sat out here on the runway waiting for you," came the shock reply "Oh hell!" I heard myself say. "Don't worry, we'll be there in twenty minutes," came the always calm and cheery response.

Like that Birmingham Mail Newspaper lecturer, who had called me a sub's dream, all those years ago, Aspro quickly became my dream client because once certain guidelines had been agreed, they virtually gave me carte blanche to exploit every positive media opportunity I could, to raise their profile both regionally and nationally.

Every time the company announced a new holiday destination from Cardiff, Bristol, or Belfast, there was a news story which the media would virtually always use and with an airline as a client, there were always interesting and newsy things going on.

I started making fortnightly, and later weekly, visits to Aspro House to wander around putting my head around the doors of various departments to find out what was going on.

I soon got to know all the key personnel, some of whom were to remain friends for many years to come, and invariably picked up a fresh story.

It was very like doing my old district news reporter's job all over again, but this time with a client company for a patch.

It all seemed to be going so well until a Middle East dictator called, Saddam Hussein, decided to invade Kuwait.

I learnt of the surprise invasion on the car radio as we drive home from a lovely family holiday weekend at Hartland Quay in North Devon.

It was August 1990 and I had now been handling the Aspro media publicity for a year, but I did not realise the implications of this far-away military incursion across the desert sands, for Aspro and for me.

It suddenly became all too clear, a few days later with an early morning call from Aspro.

Cyprus with its two British air bases at Akrotiri and Dhekelia, was poised to play a strategic role in any Allied counter offensive operations in the Middle East and ABTA, the Association of British Travel Agents, had suggested that holidaymakers should think twice before going there.

Aspro had diversified its destinations in recent years, but Cyprus was still crucially important to its operations and, to make matters worse, some operators had already started cancelling flights to the Eastern Mediterranean island.

Aspro had one distinct advantage because having its own airline it had no reliance on other carriers and could make its own decision.

The Foreign Office had yet to put out an official notice advising British nationals not to go to Cyprus, so Aspro decided to keep on flying.

But the situation suddenly changed and when it became clear that in the event of a rapid escalation of military flights, air space for holiday jets could not be guaranteed, the decision was taken to bring clients home and to suspend further departures for the time being.

Within hours, the telephones at Aspro House began ringing off the hook with hundreds of people calling in and wanting to know if they were going to be offered alternatives, and others protesting because they did not want to be brought home, or because they still wanted to go anyway.

It was not long before the local press, first in Cardiff and then in Bristol and Belfast, picked up on the story and my phone started non-stop ringing.

All the newspapers, which I had exploited endlessly in my drive for Aspro coverage, were now even more keen to print this story because it gave them a strong local angle on an international crisis.

It was a pretty straight forward issue, from the Aspro point of view, because the company had acted in the best interest of its clients in a situation over which it had absolutely no control and certainly could not be criticised for putting safety before its own commercial considerations.

My situation was also helped because I already had a good working relationship with most of the journalists, who called and there was the unspoken understanding that today's hot news, was always tomorrows chip paper.

If one was less than helpful to the Gentlemen of the Press, then when you needed a favour, they might not be quite so forthcoming and, by the same token, if they give your client a particularly hard time by not putting both sides of the argument, then one was likely to remember that.

Our Cyprus news storm soon blew over as the media quickly swept on to other more pressing issues and promptly forgot all about us.

But my roller coaster ride was only just beginning as I quickly discovered with yet another early morning call from Aspro.
-The International Leisure Group (ILG) had suddenly, collapsed, leaving thousands of pre booked Mediterranean holidays up for grabs.

All their clients were covered by the ABTA bond, so it was now a question of Aspro and other tour operators diving in piranha-like to swallow up as many of these packages as they could.

I literally leapt into action, arranging a press conference at Aspro House for 11am, followed by another one at Bristol Airport in the early afternoon.

It was an "Aspro to the Rescue," story and I knew the media would simply lap it up because again it gave them a strong local angle on a national story.

First, I called up the BBC TV Wales and HTV News Desks, quickly followed by their Bristol colleagues, because it was vitally important to get on to their daily news schedules before it was too late.

Then I called all the regional evening and morning papers and the local radio stations before jumping into the car and driving over to Cardiff to handle the 11am Head Office Press briefing, which was virtually a full house, as was the one held at Bristol Airport later that afternoon.

Aspro was rewarded by blanket coverage in all the regional media, including some earlier Inter European Airways film footage shown on HTV Wales, which was particularly pleasing.

From then on Aspro's fortunes soared with year-on-year expansion to fly to holiday destinations all around the Mediterranean from additional UK airports, including Birmingham, East Midlands, Exeter, Leeds Bradford, Newcastle, Glasgow, Edinburgh, and Inverness.

I was now generating a considerable amount of positive PR for Aspro, but things did not always go to plan.

I almost came unstuck on one memorable occasion when I called the HTV Wales News Desk at 7.30 am to see if we were on their morning schedule for a press conference about the company's expansion plans,

"Haven't you heard the news? came the chilling response. "Gorbachev has been detained while on holiday in the Crimea, so I don't expect there will be much regional news today."

One has just got to be philosophical on such occasions because you can make all the arrangements you like, but there is always the chance you will be blown away by a suddenly breaking sensational news story.

As it turned out we still got a television cameraman as well reporters from the South Wales Echo and Western Mail.

It soon became glaringly obvious that because of the increasing demands of the holiday business, and the on-going publicity needs of my other clients, I had completely outgrown Mum's back bedroom.

What was required now, was a proper office and some journalistic back-up.

The office requirement was filled when I soon found two large unfurnished rooms at, The Garage House, in the centre of the nearby picturesque village of Wrington with, better still, two inns just a few steps away, but now there was a need to find some furnishings.

While I had been heavily involved with Aspro, there had been dramatic changes on the heavily-indebted Port of Bristol front.

Here ports industry entrepreneurs, Terence Mordaunt, and David Ord, with their company, First Corporate Shipping Ltd, had stepped in and bought the entire complex, together with a large dock estate, on a one-hundred-and fifty-year lease, from the city council for some £30 million.

Inevitably there was a lot of down-sizing going on, so I was able to go into the port offices in Avonmouth and pick up four very large and pretty old-fashioned desks, complete with drawers, for a few pounds.

Digressing from Aspro for a few moments, I was, of course, well-aware of what was going on behind the scenes in the port in the year running up to the sale and had several meetings with Terence and David, who continued to retaining my services for a year after the deal was done back in 1991.

Now having acquired and furnished my office, I needed some editorial support and heard on the journo grape vine, that my former Evening Post colleague, Paul Fluck, was about to retire.

Ironically, it was Paul who had given me my new boy's tour on my first day at the old Post offices in Silver Street.

We met for lunch at the Bristol Marriott Hotel in April, 1992, and he readily agreed to come and help me out at Media-Consult.

I could not have made a better choice, because Paul always paid great attention to detail and was not easily phased by situations as he proved during his very first hour with me.

An Inter European jet had been chartered by the British Government to bring a large party of Bosnians back to the UK, so he was soon on the telephone to the British Embassy in Sarajevo, seeking the latest information for our press release.

As Aspro continued expanding, so did our workload. Paul and I would write press releases to announce new departure airports and we virtually always achieved good coverage, because no regional newspaper could resist our "Airport wins new Airline" stories or "Airport has new holiday destination-thanks to Aspro," pieces.

Every time Inter European chartered in a new aircraft, we would hold a press conference at Aspro House and then follow it up with "Holiday firm increases jet capacity from x, y and z airports," which meant we could blitz all our regions with localised releases.

As I explained earlier, having an airline as a client gave us some brilliant PR opportunities.

We arranged for older students from the various departure airport areas to be an air steward or stewardess for the day as a work experience project and then invited their local media along to cover the event which always resulted in some great feature pieces.

I asked the always obliging IEA operations team how many people it would take to tow a jet with a rope and whether we could organise a sponsored pull for charity.

They happily gave us the go-ahead and we arranged runway jet pulls in Cardiff and Bristol, with 20 local travel agents taking on Aspro and IEA staff with the local media in attendance to film and picture the highly unusual, and therefore topical event.

Aspro's announcement of its first transatlantic departures to Florida, direct from Bristol Airport, gave us one of our greatest PR opportunities, but the whole publicity operation almost become unstuck at the eleventh hour.

Paul and I went to town. We located and invited an American girls' marching band, found an American car owners club, who obligingly came along with their huge vehicles, and laid on Bucks Fizz and other entertainment for the holidaymakers checking in.

We had a full media turn-out for the early morning departure and all was going with a swing when I suddenly noticed the first wisps of fog closing in.

"Oh no this just can't be happening to me now," I muttered.

Bristol was prone to becoming fog-bound, but there had only been a light mist in the air when I left my home in nearby Congresbury at 6am.

It seemed to be getting worse, so I found Airport Director Les Wilson and voiced my fears.

Our whole Aspro message was about flying people on holiday from your own local airport, so it would be a complete PR disaster if we had to turn around and bus everyone to Birmingham, with the local media all there to report it.

Les confided that it was indeed becoming a little touch and go as weather conditions did indeed appear to be worsening, so I should cross my fingers and hope for the best.

Thankfully none of the punters had got wind of the little drama unfolding in their midst and were left in blissful ignorance when, to my huge relief, the jet finally touched down.

But we were always hostages to fortune because with Aspro and IEA now carrying more than 900,000 people on holiday every year, it was inevitable that we would also face some challenging situations.

On one such occasion, an IEA Boeing 737, took off from Crete in the early hours and as the red-coated stewardesses were beginning their in-flight service, out popped a mouse!

By chance the girl, who spotted the tiny stowaway had previously been a veterinary nurse, so instead of letting out a scream and leaping for the nearest seat, she calmly made a grab for the tiny creature, but missed and it quickly disappeared under a seat.

The Captain was immediately informed and he radioed ahead to Newcastle Airport that he would be landing with an extra passenger, whom it was assumed, had somehow hitched a ride during the boarding process.

Somewhere along the chain of command, the mouse became a rat and when the jet touched down, health officials were there to meet it, which inevitably caused a delay.

Someone tipped off the local Press and by midday this bizarre story had grown with the telling, so much so, that a rabid rat had now been terrorising a jetliner at 30,000 feet.

Paul and I received a deluge of calls and went to great lengths to explain that the stowaway had been a mouse and not a rat, and that no one had been bitten or had even known of the presence of the tiny creature until after the aircraft had landed.

There then followed an operational knock-on effect because the aircraft had to be taken out of service and fumigated and this led to inevitable delays affecting other inbound and outbound flights because no airline can afford to keep a spare jet on 24-7 standby as a replacement.

Aspro's always frantically busy marketing department would be working on the production of holiday brochures months in advance, so much so that Paul and I would be writing stories on new winter destinations in the spring and producing new summer releases before the current holiday season had even ended.

Tempting the media to write about autumn and winter before September 1st or spring and summer before January 1st was always a challenge, but we were usually able to hit the mark if we could announce a brand-new destination or a big increase in flights.

Another great way we were able to win thousands of column inches for Aspro and promote the brochures was on the back of mini feature stories called "A day in the Life of a Holiday Rep."

The temptation for busy Features Editors to give a good show to a professionally-written story with pictures of a lad or lass from their patch working overseas, and in the sun, was usually irresistible.

Once Aspro had approved the publicity idea that I should send someone out to do a series of interviews and the Marketing Department had decided upon the most strategically-valuable areas, then I would go to see Aspro's always enthusiastic Overseas Manager, Debbie Taylor.

Liverpool-born Debbie, had worked her way up from rep to resort manager and had eventually returned to Cardiff to be in overall charge of all the boys and girls working overseas.

It was Debbie and her team, who arranged our ticketing and accommodation and initially liaised with resort managers on our behalf.

Paul flew off from Bristol Airport on the first of these PR exercises early one morning and, to my surprise, was on the phone to me just after 10am the following morning with a great story!

"What is it?" I asked, only to be told that an elderly guest staying at his hotel had just been found dead in bed!

"Paul that is NOT a great story and we shall keep very quiet about it" I replied.

His initial reaction was, of course, completely understandable, after more than 30 years on the Post.

As both of us were simply far too busy to spend chunks of time away interviewing Aspro reps, I co-opted a life-long friend, John Harris, to do the job.

Having said I was too busy, I always made time for a Tuesday afternoon game of golf with John on the delightful public course overlooking the sea at Portishead.

Thanks to the wonders of technology, I had my trusty mobile phone, a small brick in those days, so if there was an Aspro or some other inquiry, which Paul felt, I should handle, then he would pass the caller on to me.

It was on one such Tuesday afternoon that I asked him if he would handle the overseas job for me.

John was not a journalist, but had spent his professional life in newspaper and magazine advertising and happened to be between jobs. having recently returned from working for an agency in the Middle East, so the idea of a few weeks helping me out appealed to him.

To make the commission easier, I composed a detailed questionnaire, similar to my old, Clevedon Mercury, wedding forms, so as long as John returned with good pictures and all the questions answered, then it was dead easy for Paul and I to rattle out features.

We invariably used the same intro and body text and just changed the names and personal information and it all worked a treat

When John was "in resort," he was able to interview and picture as many as six reps on his three or four-day trips, and because they came from all over the UK, this gave us a wide, region by region, spread of good feature stories, which all carried the tail end message about flying with Aspro and IEA from your own local airport.

What was so refreshing about my media arrangement with the Aspro was that they were perfectly relaxed about giving me a free hand to use my professional knowledge and skills on their behalf, provided what was produced was accurate and in the company's best interest.

Our releases were almost always speedily approved and normally only changed to make them more accurate.
So many company bosses, or department heads, simply cannot resist the temptation of sticking their oar in and messing up perfectly good copy.

Just because they can write a sentence in English, they assume that they are good as you are.

How many times would I have loved to have said to the client: "Look, there is no way I would ever presume to tell you how to do your job, so why, oh! why, do you think you can tell me how to do mine?"

During my five-year relationship with Aspro, I realised that to run competitions in major regional newspapers with a family holiday for four as the prize, was a great way to generate half, or even whole pages of coverage, and especially if I could ensure that the competition ran for weeks on end.

So, I dreamed up The Funny Holiday Story competition, whereby readers were encouraged to write in to Media-Consult with their amusing holiday experiences, which I or, Dave Baxter, the latest recruit to my PR operations, would turn into copy for the participating newspaper and, of course, every piece would include an Aspro promo.

Dave, who came along after Paul had decided to retire to Teignmouth, was the neighbour who drove me from my then home in Portishead to the Post Head Office in Silver Street during my two week's induction.

Dave had been the Post's motoring correspondent for many years and his retirement from the paper just happened to coincide with my winning of a contract to handle publicity for the Castle Combe racing circuit in Wiltshire.

So, when Dave, who occupied one of the Port of Bristol desks in my outer office, was not busy writing press releases about forthcoming track days, he was free to lend a hand with Aspro.

So back to those funny holiday stories sent in by readers, and to one about a South Wales couple, who were flying out from Cardiff on their first ever self-catering holiday.

They had d borrowed a cool bag from a neighbour, which they packed full of food and handed in with their cases.

Not long after, they were called back to the check-in desk to find their bag, which had burst open, now on the counter.

"Does this bag belong to you madam? because when I saw three pork pies, followed by a large block of cheese and tins of ham coming along the conveyor belt, I thought I was back in the supermarket!" said this busy baggage handling supervisor, who was not amused.

A young couple told how they had borrowed a tent to go on their first ever camping holiday and had great difficulty securing it to their roof rack because the wooden poles seemed rather large.

When they arrived late at this camping site and were struggling to erect it, a couple of other campers came over to help and pointed out that their tent was actually a small marquee!" this reader explained.

But all was well which ends well because someone else loaned the couple a small two-person tent and their marquee became a community space for the week.

But inevitably, all good PR things come to an end, and it was on the last evening of ABTA's annual conference in Palma, Majorca, that I received the first indication that the Aspro business, as I knew it would finally be coming to an end.

I had succeeded in getting the company on to the front page of the conference newspaper with the news that Aspro was planning flights to Egypt and was sitting in a bar with company colleagues, including Aspro's energetic Northern Regional Director, Trevor Davis, when it was hinted that the company might be sold.

The rationale was simple - both Thomson Holidays, the long-established market leader, and their main rival, Airtours, were supported by huge chains of group-owned travel agencies with which the likes of Aspro could not compete.

Aspro had grown just about as far as it could under its own steam, so it made sound commercial sense to sell the brand to one of the major players.

Ironically, again it was an early morning call from Aspro, which brought final confirmation that the company had just been sold to Airtours.

An announcement was being made to the staff at 11am and I was asked to fix a press Conference for 2pm.

I quickly called up all the regional media with the news that a major statement was to made and then hurried over to Cardiff for the 11am meeting.

The main hall was crowded to the doors with staff members when the new owners were introduced, and the following press conference was also a jam-packed affair.

I was thanked for all my hard work, for which of course I had been extremely well paid, and the new owners were strongly recommended to take on my services.

But I instinctively knew that things were never going to be quite the same again, and that this was going to be the beginning of the end.

Some key Aspro personnel did decide to go their own way, rather than joining Airtours, and were soon offering me exciting new PR opportunities, but the writing was on the wall.

I did go on working with Airtours for a few months, at a substantially reduced fee, and was invited up to the company's head office in Rossendale, a small town in Lancashire.
There the then sales and marketing director indicated that they were looking for a new Head of PR and would I like the job?

I was flattered by the surprise offer, but politely declined.

NEW BEGINNINGS & THE BIG SLEEP YEARS

When Airtours acquired Aspro, Debbie Taylor, the Overseas Manager, who had helped organise my occasional overseas PR trips, decided to leave the company and became Sales and Marketing Manager of the Copthorne Hotel at, Culverhouse Cross, on the western outskirts of the city.

She suggested to General Manager, Simon Reed, that I should be taken on to do the hotel's press and publicity.

Simon, who had been minded to employ a local PR company, invited me in for an interview and after Debbie and I had been bouncing publicity ideas around for 20 minutes or so, getting more and more excited about what could be achieved, he promptly gave me the job.

Debbie and I met for a light lunch on a monthly basis, with me always choosing a prawn sandwich on brown bread with a pint of lager shandy, and during these sessions we came up with all sorts of publicity stunts.

The hotel overlooked a small lake enclosed within its grounds, but its population of ducks was diminishing nightly, courtesy of a family of urban foxes, who had grown rather partial to duck pate, and other such dishes.

We decided to provide our feathered friends with a portable radio in the hope that the nocturnal music would scare of the hungry predators.

"Will the ducks be tuned in to our station?" a local BBC Wales reporter asked, when I called up give him the story.

"Well of course," was the obvious response. I don't recall whether or not we saved the poor old ducks, but we certainly got some great publicity.

In one of our more bizarre moments, we put out a press appeal for a gondola so that wedding couples would have a romantic setting for their photographs and then went one better by offering to stage a local windsurfing competition on our water.

When Debbie went on to become, Head of Sales and Marketing, at the rival Marriott Hotel in the centre of Cardiff, the new Copthorne General Manager Brian McCarthy asked me if I had any plans to accompany her.

"Of course not, Brian, because my contract is with you and not with Debbie," I replied.

"Well in that case, would you also be prepared to do some PR for the Cardiff Hoteliers Association, although we could not pay you a great deal?" came his surprise response.

This offer was, to quote an oft-used expression, a 'no brainer,' because it immediately opened the door to a whole raft of potential new clients, and in truth, I would have taken on this commission for nothing.

Over the next few months, I drove over to Cardiff and met the general managers of all the city hotels, including, Cormac O'Keefe, who headed up the Jurys Doyle Hotel in the centre of town.

Cormac took me on and, in turn, recommended my services to his opposite number, Con Ring, GM of the Jurys waterfront hotel, just off Bristol City Centre, and only a 30-minute drive from my office in Wrington.

So, as if by magic, my PR wheel had turned full circle and I went on to work with Con for many years to come, both in Bristol and in London.

I was also taken on by, Stephen Godber, GM of Cardiff's much smaller Quality Friendly Hotel and worked with him for a short while until he moved on.

I could never have known it at the time, but when Stephen suddenly popped up in my professional life in a phone call a couple of years later, it was to have the most amazing consequences.

"Hi Nigel. I am back in Cardiff at a brand-new hotel and I was wondering if you would like to come over to Cardiff to meet the owner?" was the intriguing, out-of-the-blue invitation, I received from Stephen one morning in 1999.

The former British Gas headquarters, a nine-storey tower block in the centre of the city, had been converted into an 81-bedroom hotel, but then acquired by the Bedfactory Hotel Group.

The hotel stood on concrete piers with parking and Reception on the ground floor and birds eye views over the busy main road below.

Stephen welcomed me and led me into an inner office, where Cosmo Fry, a descendant of the famous Frys Chocolate family. walked into my life and would become a close client for the next nine years.

Cosmo, it seemed, had got to know Hollywood star John Malkovich, when they were neighbours in Provence, and John had agreed to invest in Cosmo's plan to create a new and refreshing brand of budget hotels with chic.

With the enthusiastic and untiring support of his business partner, Lulu Anderson, a former national newspaper fashion journalist, who was later to become his wife, Cosmo had just turned his concept for an affordable hotel with style, elegance, and sophistication into a reality.

It was to be named The Big Sleep and, as Stephen gave me a tour around, I was already thinking that it would be a dream to promote.

The hotel was a symphony in blue and white, with distinctive fleece curtains and Formica furnishings made at Cosmo's small factory in Bath he had set up with the help of his famous father, Jeremy, friend of Princess Margaret and Lord Snowdon.

Now synchronicity was to play its part and create one of the biggest PR opportunities of my career, because it just so happened, that the weird and wonderful movie, Being John Malkovich, had just been released.

The star had agreed to fly in to Cardiff and officially open The Big Sleep and secretaries from all over the city had been invited to come in and have breakfast with him!

It was clever plan as Cosmo had realised that in those pre-internet days it was the secretaries, who booked accommodation for their employers' clients visiting the city and therefore it would be good to have them on his side.

And here my Lady Luck played her part, because I had recently been joined at Media-Consult by my friend, fellow journalist, and walking companion of many years, Peter Gibbs, former Assistant Editor of my earlier rival newspaper, the Western Daily Press.

Peter was gifted with a flair for organising imaginative news-led promotions and a few years earlier had created the Archers' fictional village of Ambridge in Warwickshire and laid on a coach for competition-winning readers to travel there and meet the actors playing their parts.

So putting in place all the arrangements to make the very most of this publicity coup was right up his professional street.

Cosmo and Lulu gave us a free hand to make the most of this PR gift of an opportunity of promoting their new Big Sleep brand, and I think I can honestly say that Peter did not disappoint.

By the time John flew in to Cardiff Airport, Peter had arranged a live slot on Channel Four's then-flagship Big Breakfast Show to be followed by a whole series of media interviews.

And if that was not enough, it had also been arranged for John to don 'baby blue' pyjamas, referencing the hotel's main corporate colour, and climb into a big bed in the hotel's spacious foyer, from where he would meet and greet the star-struck secretaries.

The afternoon that Peter and I pressed the lift button which took us up to the ninth floor to meet the world-famous actor, who was just settling in to the penthouse suite was one that neither of us will ever forget.

Within minutes, John had happily agreed to fall in with Peter's schedule of interview arrangements and we were on our way back down in the lift with him - now surprisingly joined by a national newspaper photographer, who took a picture of the three of us.

Cosmo and Lulu, who were also very media-minded, had arranged to receive dozens of Being John Malkovich face masks, which were put to extremely good use.

But my constant companion, the Cosmic Joker, could not resist doing his best to throw his small spanner into the works and did so almost immediately after Cosmo and Lulu had taken John and their fellow investors out for supper!

The centrepiece of all Peter's carefully-prepared PR plans, which had worked like a dream up until now, was to be John's slot on The Big Breakfast Show.

Presenter Richard Bacon had already arrived and the plan was for him to act as a bell boy in the morning when John pretended to check in.

All was thrown into doubt by a call from the crew of the mobile TV unit with its communications dish, who were now below manoeuvring amid the hotel's giant concrete support pilers, trying desperately to find a spot from where they could receive a clear signal.

Should they fail, then that would be that, and there would be no Big Breakfast Show with its morning audience, which went on to top a record two million viewers the following year.

I hurried down the hotel's entrance ramp and watched their continued manoeuvrings with my heart thumping and then, thank God, a thumbs-up hand appeared from the rig!

All went like a PR dream the following morning with John pretending to check in and Bell Boy Richard playing his part.

The producers had cleverly provided a pair of spectacles for the star to wear, with a tiny camera in the bridge-piece, so at Reception and on a later walk-about meeting passers-by outside the hotel, viewers were able to Be John Malkovich.

There then followed an on-the-sofa interview with John, which was going so well that The Big Breakfast Show presenters returned to pick up with The Big Sleep, several more times during the course of the programme, which was a bonus.

And the secretaries, of course, were thrilled to get up close and personal with a Hollywood icon.

But then there was another surprise, which neither Peter nor I had expected with the sudden appearance of Welsh rock band, the Manic Street Preachers, who had turned up to meet John.

Then, ever willing, he took yet another media call from one of the national radio stations on the way back to Cardiff Airport and his flight back to resuming filming his next movie in Spain.

It was while having one of our regular update briefings with Cosmo that the subject of finding a property suitable for conversion into a second Big Sleep hotel was raised and we came up with a cunning plan, which to our surprise, quickly produced a result.

I wrote a news release saying that entrepreneur Cosmo Fry, whose investor friends included famous Hollywood actor, John Malkovich, was looking for a building to convert into a second Big Sleep Hotel in a city, with the name of the target city or towns to be inserted.

I sent that out to all the major regional papers around the country and within weeks, Cosmo received a call from an estate agency in Cheltenham, saying that he thought the former ten-storey, Apsley House, a redundant 1970s Inland Revenue building in the centre of the famous Regency spa town would prove ideal for conversion into an hotel, and so it proved to be.

While Cosmo and Lulu literally rolled up their sleeves and became totally hands-on with the Cheltenham conversion project it. also became our main PR preoccupation for months to come, as far as The Big Sleep was concerned.

Peter even arranged for an independent TV production company to make a six-part series called, Risky Business, which followed Cosmo and Lulu, like a fly on the wall, as the project progressed, and was to be broadcast on the then HTV.

We also made numerous visits to Cheltenham, where we liaised with the Borough Council's most helpful marketing department, getting involved with Cheltenham In Bloom and even arranging for Big Sleep banners to appear on the main road into town.

On the grand opening day in 2006, my Cosmic Joker finally woke up after quite a long sleep and decided to lob yet another of his spanners into the works.

Peter had arranged for a local helicopter operator to pick up Cosmo and best-selling author Jilly Cooper, who he had known for many years, from Staverton Airport and land them in the nearby grounds of Cheltenham Ladies College, where there was to be a ceremonial tree planting followed by a signing of Jilly's latest book during the celebration reception back at the hotel.

I left home early and as I drove up the M5 towards Cheltenham, the weather began slowly deteriorating and I began wondering if it would prevent the helicopter from taking off and so 'ground' all our arrangements.

It was a complete deja vu of the morning fog which almost prevented the Inter European holiday jet landing at Bristol Airport to fly Aspro holidaymakers to the USA.

But thankfully, all went well, and the helicopter landed to a big welcome from Cheltenham Girls' School students, who had been lined up at a safe distance from the helicopter's designated landing area.

From Cheltenham, Cosmo's Bedfactory Hotel Company, went on to acquire the Wish Tower Hotel on Eastbourne's King Edward's Parade, sitting opposite the famous Martello Tower on the foreshore and within easy walking distance of the town centre.

The Big Sleep Eastbourne opened in the summer of 2008 and was the finale project with which Media-Consult was involved and included bringing a Punch and Judy Show into the foyer on the grand reopening day.

So ended a nine-year professional engagement with Cosmo and Lulu who were by that time, more friends than clients.

So much was going on, pretty much at the same time, in my PR operation, that I must admit, that after the passage of so many years, I am finding it quite difficult to arrange all the happenings in the correct order, but may be this is the place to write about the ship repair industry and my small part in promoting it.

During my hectic ten years covering the Port of Bristol for the Post, while at the same time carrying on my freelance activities, I contacted the Swansea dry dock company.

I drove down the M4 on a day off to interview its General Manager, Jim Eccles, and produce the first of a regular supply of story releases for Lloyds.

Not long after I had left the Post, I had an out-of-the-blue call from Jim telling me that he had moved on from Swansea and was now GM of the Harland and Wolff ship repair company in Belfast and would I like to fly over so that we could discuss the handling of the company's PR.

This was some years before the signing of the historic Good Friday Agreement, so I had to admit to having some thoughts of trepidation as on my taxi drove me from the airport to the port and I could not help noticing several results of 'the troubles.'

The idea of promoting a ship repair company, based overlooking the very same dock in which the ill-fated Titanic had been built, certainly excited me and I willingly accepted Jim's PR commission.

Every nine weeks from then, I would fly from Bristol to Belfast for an update meeting with Jim, over a pub lunch, from which I went on to produce a whole raft of releases for the shipping and ship repair publications

This routine continued for a couple of years until circumstances changed and this most interesting contract had run its course.

TREASURE ISLAND

It all began in the shower on a Christmas afternoon as I half listened to Robert Louis Stevenson's wonderful story of Treasure Island on our bedroom radio, while getting ready for our traditional family festive supper.

Why had no one in Bristol ever capitalised on that great swashbuckling adventure, a little voice in my head asked?

After all, the treasure seeking ship, Hispaniola, with her black-hearted cook, Long John Silver, cabin boy hero, Jim Hawkins, and the rest of the crew, had sailed out of Bristol on a great voyage of adventure that was to captivate and enthral generations of children around the world.

Wouldn't it be great to have a Treasure Island-themed attraction, where kids could clamber over a pirate ship and dig for treasure in a tropical lagoon setting, my voice suggested?

Once Christmas was over, I set about raising the idea with various clients and contacts, who I thought might be interested, but to my surprise no one seemed the slightest bit enthusiastic, so I eventually forgot all about it.

But the idea suddenly and inexplicably popped right back into my head as I sat waiting at traffic lights in Bristol City Centre on my way to a lunchtime meeting with a contact, who was a marketing chief with a regional development firm.

We had first met a couple of years earlier while I was handling the publicity for a company, which had planned to bring a small Canadian cruise ship, The Princess Margarita, back to Bristol and moor her up in the city docks as a floating hotel.

My contact had been interested in his company handling any shore-side civil engineering works, which might have been required, but in the end the project never went ahead.

He had also been instrumental in Media-Consult being invited to quote for his company's then highly-lucrative PR contract, but we had not been successful.

Still, we continued to meet up from time to time and this was to be one of our lunchtime catch-up chats.

Once we had ordered a sandwich and settled down with a drink in the lounge bar of the Bristol Marriott City Centre Hotel, where I had first talked to Paul about joining me, I got out my notebook, turned it broadside and began drawing a dome.

"What do you think of this?" I asked, proceeding to draw a sailing ship inside the bubble and a tropical beach, complete with treasure chest.

My friend was immediately enthusiastic about my Treasure Island idea and to my huge surprise, said he also knew of just the site for it, close to the junction of the M5 and M4 at Almondsbury.

By complete chance, he was also due to have a meeting in London the very next day with an engineering company, specialising in tensile structures, which could be suitable for our theme park dome.

He took my idea to his London meeting and by another equally big coincidence, it turned out that the MD there was interested in the history of piracy.

A couple of weeks later, he and a colleague drove down to Bristol to have a look at the proposed site with us and we then adjourned to the nearby Aztec West Hotel to work out an initial strategy.

My friend had by this time joined another Bristol-based firm and they quickly became involved in the project, and then appointed me to assist with their PR.

Over the following month, other companies and enterprising individuals were drawn into the Treasure Island enterprise on the general understanding that any services they provided in advance, and on a complimentary basis, would be rewarded when the project attracted major funding and eventually became a reality.

Media-Consult picked up still more PR work from a commercial property agency, which became involved, but I gradually drifted more to the sidelines and mostly watched as my creation went on growing and developing to become a multi-million- pound themed attraction centred on a series of all-weather domes.

By this time, we had moved on from the North Bristol site to target a large parcel of potential development land on the outskirts of Weston-super-Mare, but eventually this was also passed over in favour of hundreds of acres in the village of Magor, close to the second Severn Bridge in South Wales.

The site, partly in Newport and partly in Gwent, was ideally located to attract visitors from the Midlands and the North of England, as well as those coming over the Severn Bridge from London, the South-east and the South-west.

By this time, Legend Court, as the project company had now become known, had attracted substantial speculative funding, which enabled the purchasing of development options on all the target land.

The site was not zoned for development on the plans of either local authority, but would, if permitted, lead to the creation of thousands of local jobs as well as the generation of substantial sums in rates.

Our scheme was formally announced at a presentation held at the nearby Celtic Manor Resort's Golf and Country Club and attracted a huge amount of both regional and national publicity, as well as opposition from local people who, quite understandably, did not want a theme park in their midst.

I had now received a shareholding in the project, which, if developed to its full potential, would probably make me around £1 million better off.

I tried not to think about this too much because I still had quite a demanding business of my own to run and this was still a hugely speculative venture.

Everything hinged on a green light from the two local planning authorities, because once they had accepted the principle that the site could be developed, then it would instantly have a huge capital value, which could then easily be used to attract the substantial funds needed for the first phase.

The problem was that councillors wanted proof that there were sufficient cash available to fund the project before they would consider giving their approval.

Their argument was that once they had opened the flood gates by accepting that this large area of farm land could be developed, then they might not have any real control over what would happen there if the theme park did not proceed for one reason or another.

In a bid to meet the councillors' stipulations, a phased funding package was arranged through US interests and a special meeting of Newport Council planners was fixed for the week before Christmas.

I travelled over on the train because I had no desire to do battle with city centre parking, when I could simply walk to the council offices from the station.

It was a nostalgic ride down memory lane because as the train plunged deep into Brunel's Severn Tunnel, I suddenly remembered the week I spent on holiday in Newport with a close teenage friend and staying in a family friend's terraced house in Victoria Avenue.

The Newport Council Planning Committee meeting room was already almost full when I arrived and I soon identified a small contingent from the Magor Residents' Action Group.

Everyone settled down, the Chairman called the meeting to order and the proceedings opened with a strong statement of support from the Council's Economic Development Officer.

Councillors rose to speak, one after another and as the deliberations gradually unfolded, it became painfully obvious to me that the overall weight of the argument was coming down in favour of a rejection.

I sat there, completely helpless, listening and watching as two years of intense work and negotiations by a lot of people, many of whom had given all their time and efforts for nothing, slowly, but inexorably came to nought.

The Committee rejected the application by a majority and members of the Action Group produced a bottle of champagne to toast their local success.

With substantial job losses in the South Wales steel industry looming, I could not help thinking that councillors had missed the golden opportunity of creating literally thousands of new jobs and the generation of millions of pounds in spin-off work for companies in the region.

Walking back down the hill to the station with signs of festive cheer all around me, I felt more sad than disappointed, because such a great opportunity had been simply thrown away.

Maybe if I had got more involved winning hearts and minds at a local level, then perhaps the outcome might have been different, I mused.

But it was too late now because I knew there would never be sufficient funds to lodge a formal appeal, brief a barrister and prepare for a full-scale Public Enquiry, which could take anything up to two years to come. to a public hearing.

Still, it was simply amazing just how far one could go with a single good idea.

I had made quite a lot of money in PR fees along the way, I consoled myself as we again plunged into the Severn Tunnel with all the fun of a family Christmas to look forward to when we emerged at the other end.

WORKING WITH AMTRAK

While Stephen Godber was welcoming me to the Big Sleep in Cardiff, I had another new client on the go back in Bristol, and right opposite the Bristol Evening Post HQ and printing centre in Temple Way.

For there was the HQ of Amtrak Express Parcels, run by entrepreneur Roger Bains and his wife, Elaine, who had launched their fledgling business back in 1987.carrying just 40 parcels on their first night.

But from that small beginning, they had built up a parcel moving franchise business with a giant central sortation hub in the West Midlands and 120 depots right across the country.

These were run by self-employed franchisees with their own fleet of white delivery vans, complete with a distinctive red and blue Amtrak logo.

It was, of course, the same name as the USA rail company, which many years later was to carry Peter and me on two epic journeys from Chicago across the continent – to San Francisco the first time and then to Los Angeles.

I can't remember what prompted me to contact their Sales and Marketing Manager, Roger Gamlin, but he invited me into his office.

It became clear as we chatted about the business that he was not altogether happy with his present PR company and he was willing to give me a month's trial.

I had taken the trouble to do my research and suggested a couple of news story angles, which I turned into releases and were duly published.

It's funny how one remembers some things, but I was having the afternoon off and had taken my family on a cruise aboard the, MV Balmoral, from Clevedon Pier, when my mobile rang and it was Roger inviting me to take over their PR contract, which I went on to hold for the next nine years.

It so happened that, Frances Hardcastle, was standing down as Editor of my old paper, the South Avon Mercury.

I had known Frances and her husband, Bob, for some years, so I asked her if she might be interested in driving over to Wrington a couple of afternoons a week and lending me a hand with Amtrak.

Luckily for me, she was interested and remained with me for five years until deciding to go off and study for a degree.

It seems hard to believe it now, but in those days our press releases were faxed over to clients and then printed off and sent out in white envelopes, often literally dozens at a time.

I can still hear our printer clattering away machine gun-like in the background of my mind, until that is the growing introduction of emails changed everything.

Frances and I attended monthly update briefings with Roger and it was not many months after we had started, that he announced that he now wished to receive all future releases by email!

Once back in the office, I wasted no time in arranging for Media-Consult to be equipped with four sit-up-and-beg, Amstrad computers, one for each desk and all linked together, so that copy could be buzzed over from one to another, hence we entered the Internet age

Amtrak was a gift of a client because they were continually doing free A to B deliveries for charitable organisations and individuals and these always resulted in good news stories for the depots involved.

It was not long before we had built up an extensive database of all the newspapers and freelance photographers, right across the country.

Amtrak, I believe, was the only company offering a collection and delivery service for the nation's hundreds of pigeon fanciers, using specially-designed cardboard boxes, and this resulted in dozens of great news stories.

What news editor could resist a story about a racing pigeon, which failed to reach home, but was found and returned to its loft, thanks to Amtrak

Frances even found herself calling Buckingham Palace on one occasion, concerning a bird, who had failed to return to the royal loft.

On another occasion, we learnt that one of the franchisees was delivering a menagerie of larger-than-life animals made of fibreglass, from their creator to a zoo, for some special promotional occasion and this gave me an idea,

So, I called him up and commissioned him to make a large and colourful owl, whom we christened Ambrose.

From then on, if any Amtrak franchisee needed a little extra publicity support, we would have him deliver our ambassador owl to his local library where, back in those days, the local librarian was only too willing to lay on a book reading for children on the understanding that we would have a picture taken for the local paper.

But without doubt, our most successful awareness raising exercise, to which I returned time and again over my nine years with Amtrak, was the simple five or six paragraph 'Business Up' story, which proved irresistible to regional newspaper Business Editors all over the country.

"Business is on the up and up in Manchester, according to the local depot of nationwide parcels carrier. Amtrak, who are reporting a twenty per cent rise in deliveries over the past three months," would run the story intro.

And, as you will have probably already guessed, we simply changed the name of the town or city and mailed the piece out all over the country to be rewarded with a confetti-like shower of cuttings.

It seems hard to imagine it now, but PR companies back in those, dawn of the Internet days, had to supply their clients with actual newspaper and magazine cuttings to prove their worth and one could even subscribe to cuttings agencies to carry out this then essential task

But it was the free deliveries or collections for charity, which gave us a, once in a lifetime story.

For working quietly away in his Swansea home, was one, Tony Evans, who was intent on creating the world's largest rubber band ball!

As the story captured the public imagination, parcels of brown rubber bands started arriving from all over the country, even including from the Post Office, and we produced regular reports as Tony's ball grew and grew.

He knotted together some six million bands over five years and finally stopped when the giant ball weighed 2,600ibs, as was confirmed after my colleague, Peter, had arranged an official Guinness Book of Records weigh-in at Cardiff's Millenium Stadium.

But having taken the world record, what was now become of the ball - that was a question that Peter and Tony pondered, having offered it to a Cardiff science museum and been turned down?

Then, right out of the blue, an American museum attraction company, called, Ripley's Believe It or Not!, called Tony and offered to take the ball on a publicity tour around the USA on a purpose-built perspex-covered trailer before dropping it from a great height over Arizona's Mojave desert - to see just how high it would bounce.

It was an offer that Tony and his wife, Liz, could not refuse and the couple were flown out to Arizona to watch the spectacular event.

But the result was not quite what had been expected.

Instead of bouncing, the ball, which had a 14ib 8oz circumference, fell to Earth at an estimated speed of 400mph, crashed into the sun-baked earth and created a giant crater, leaving pieces of rubber bands scattered far and wide.

Tony had earlier presented Peter with a mini ball mounted on a block as a token of his thanks for all his support, and it took pride of place on a shelf in our office.

But like that rubber band ball, all good things finally come to an end and not long afterwards, Roger Bains, sold his company and so ended our long association with Amtrak Express Parcels.

ROCCO FORTE HOTELS & TRANSUN

My former Aspro Holidays and Copthorne Hotel friend, Debbie Taylor, popped back into my business life again with the news that she had moved on from Marriott and had now been appointed, Sales and Marketing Director, of Rocco Forte's flagship and exclusive waterfront, St David's Hotel and Spa, and would like me to come over to talk about PR.

Peter accompanied me, and while we were chatting in the hotel's coffee lounge, Debbie told us that she would very much like to see the hotel publicised in some national glossy magazines.

"I think we might be able to help with that," responded Peter, immediately putting on his former, Western Daily Press, Assistant Editor's innovative promotions hat.

Debbie promptly agreed to his suggestion that the hotel should offer a competition prize of a two-night break in one of the hotel's luxurious Master Suites.

This was coupled with a reader offer – book a B&B stay and be upgraded to the same spacious accommodation as would be enjoyed by the prize-winner.

Back in the office, Peter called up a target magazine, whose promotions editor promptly agreed to run the contest-offer on a full editorial page with no advertising fee charged.

The promotion generated bookings of more than 30 bed nights and was then rolled out to more magazines, happy to have a luxury prize for their readers..

Debbie was delighted and promptly recommended us to her opposite number at Rocco Forte's recently-opened Lowry Hotel, overlooking the Salford Quays in Manchester.

Peter and I then made the first of many regular visits by train from Bristol Temple Meads station and were then also recommended to Rocco's landmark Balmoral Hotel in Edinburgh.

Then, one afternoon in 2002 and right out of the blue, to our surprise, we were also contacted by the General Manager of Sir Rocco's exclusive Astoria Hotel in the centre of St Petersburg, inviting us to fly in for a meeting!

Here synchronicity was again to play its part. My former Aspro colleague and friend, Trevor Davis, who had been with me in that Majorcan bar on that momentous night when it was hinted that the company might be sold, had, like Debbie, decided to go his own way.

Trevor, a true travel industry marketing professional, and ten years younger than myself, had gone on to head up the marketing for, Transun, the long-established daybreak tour operator, and Media-Consult was duly appointed to handle the PR and had been doing so for some time.

Transun was and still is a major player in day flights from UK regional airports to Lapland to meet Father Christmas, which naturally resented us with plenty of seasonal PR gifts.

But it also offered European city day breaks, including one to St Petersburg.

So, the company willingly agreed to book Peter and myself on a flight from London Gatwick to the famous Russian city.

We left the office in Wrington around 4pm, drove to Gatwick and checked in at The Marriott and there treated ourselves to a good dinner in preparation for an early night, as our Transun flight was due to take off at 6am the following morning.

We had just finished dinner when my mobile rang with the news from our main Transun contact, that their Gatwick to St Petersburg flight had yet to be confirmed, because of an ongoing row between the UK airport and the Russian authorities, and was highly likely to be cancelled!

"But our 6am departure from Manchester has been confirmed, so do you want to switch flights?" she asked.

Peter and I looked at one another and, without hesitation said 'Yes, please,' because this was too good a PR opportunity to miss and, besides, the Astoria General Manager was expecting us.

We checked out with me thinking that I had earlier enjoyed my most expensive bath ever!

By 1am, Peter, who was driving, was beginning to flag, and we knew we just had to find somewhere to stop, so we pulled in at the Stafford Services on the M6, which were just up ahead.

By great good fortune, the adjoining lodge was still open and we managed put our heads down for a few hours.

But we miscalculated our departure time and were back on the M6 with only just enough time to complete the one hour, 45-minute drive to Manchester Airport and worse was to come!

For as we drove into the airport complex, we suddenly realised we had no idea whether we should be heading for terminals one, two or three, and with less than an hour to go, making the wrong choice would result in us missing the flight!

Then we spotted a hotel entrance and, braking hard, Peter swerved in and sped up to the entrance, where I leapt out, ran into a deserted foyer, and looked anxiously about me.

Luckily, the night porter suddenly appeared and told me we needed terminal two.
Once back in the car, there was no alternative, but to drive straight into the multi-storey short stay car park.

From there, it was a short dash into the terminal and up to the check-in desk, where we discovered that no one had told the staff we were switching flights from Gatwick to Manchester.

However after another long run through, what seemed like endless passages, looking out frantically for direction signs, we finally reached the, St Petersburg, gate, in the nick of time.

"Another minute and we would all have gone from here", a member of the ground team, told us.

All the other passengers were already belted in as we hurried along the cabin and collapsed into two empty seats at the back.

Once we had reached cruising height and the seatbelt signs had been switched off, I ordered two glasses of Champagne.

I think I can say that after being met in Arrivals by a giant of a man called, Igor, and chauffeur-driven in a black limo to the luxurious five-star Astoria, across the way from St Isaacs Cathedral and Square, our never-to-be-forgotten day in St Petersburg was for me, a somewhat surreal affair.

The hotel, opened in 1912, reflected the glamour of the period and it was said that Hitler had planned to have a celebration ball should he have succeeded in conquering the city - then Stalingrad.

I have a memory of huge potted palms around the large tiled reception area, where we presented our credentials and were told that a suite had been set aside for us to rest before joining the General Manager for lunch.

It was clear he had been impressed with all that we had achieved for Rocco Forte Hotels in the UK and was willing to see if we could generate some business for The Astoria.

Lunch was followed by a chauffeur-driven conducted tour of St Petersburg with a highly enthusiastic guide in full flow, as we took in the various famous city sights.

She was sitting beside the driver and turning around in her seat, directed her attention at me, while Peter sat quietly out of sight.

Peter enjoying dinner in The Astoria

We dined in the beautifully-appointed restaurant where three musicians entertained us, as there were few other guests around, before being driven back to the airport for our flight home.

Sadly, despite Peter's best efforts, few of our glossy magazine readers were tempted to take up The Astoria's special offer, despite the accompanying competition, organised with our long-standing travel company friends, Travelsmith, and after six months it was decided to call it a day.

OUR OTHER HOTEL YEARS

When the then General Manager of Cardiff's Jury's Doyle Hotel recommended my services to his colleague, in Bristol, it set off a chain reaction.

For following a meeting with group marketeers, who had flown in from Dublin and met us in the Jurys South Kensington property, we were able to upload our, by now, tried and tested and highly effective competition and reader offer formula to more than ten other group properties in cities across the country.

I use the phrase 'upload' because it was a private joke between Peter and I that we were uploading a virus, which later down the line, some new Marketing Director would come in and sweep away.

But we were gone on to do promotions for Bristol's Grand Hotel and the Bristol Marriott Royal, on College Green, and City Centre.

Some years earlier, and with so much going on, it had become clear to me that I also needed some hands-on administrative back-up and this was provided with the arrival of Kerry Bee, Media-Consult's super-efficient, 'Girl Friday,' who lived with her then young family in the nearby village of Sandford.

Besides our highly successful reader offers, I developed the Jurys/Bristol Evening Post Business Person of the Month formula, which went on to run for nine years.

This was reliant on my sourcing a monthly business person from the Bristol business community, often with the assistance of the city's Chamber of Commerce.

He or she was then invited to lunch and their story, which I would have written, duly appeared on the paper's business pages.

Jurys then staged an annual gala dinner at which our overall Business Person of the Year was announced.

It really was a win, win, situation because the Post got a prestigious awards programme without having to devote any editorial support to it, the hotel was guaranteed monthly profile-raising publicity, and Media-Consult was paid by the hotel for organising it.

It was also the start of my still continuing working relationship with Rob Stokes, my former Bristol United Press colleague and later Western Daily Press Editor, who very effectively acted as MC at the annual gala dinners.

CRIBBS CAUSEWAY

Whenever I had a quiet moment, I would trawl through the regional and local papers, looking for potential clients and if I spotted a business that interested me, my modus operandi was to give them a call and asked if I could speak to their PR company.

If the receptionist or whoever picked up the phone replied that they did not have one, but that Mr or Mrs So and So in marketing, looked after that sort of thing, then I would ask to be put through, because there was always the possibility that he or she was hard pressed and did not really have the time for PR.

It never took me more than a few moments to suss out the situation and if I sensed there was a green light glimmering, I would go into my, by now off-pat spiel, and say I would write to them and maybe give them a follow-up call in a few weeks.

This I never forgot to do and could go on doing for months on end, if I sensed there could be a result further down the line.

Peter was a past master at this when it came to sourcing new magazines or regional newspapers willing to accept our magazine or newspaper reader offers.

I always picked up an Evening Post at the Congresbury newsagents on my way home for tea and read it over a cuppa, again trawling for leads, because I had realised, early on in my PR career, that one had to be continually adding clients to the top of one's pile, to compensate for those falling off at the bottom for all sorts of reasons, often beyond one's control.

So, it was on one Wednesday evening in 1995, when the Post's front page was dominated by the picture of a man with a large map standing on an empty site which had the development potential for a giant new shopping centre on the edge of Bristol.

The gentleman's name was Ian Cawley and he was representing the city firm of JT Baylis.

I immediately reached for my trusty telephone directory and quickly found the company listed in the Stokes Croft area and called them up.

It was now well past 5pm and the chances were that the office was closed, but it was still worth a try and my luck was in because, Mr Cawley picked up the phone.

I introduced myself and explained I had been a Bristol Evening Post journalist for many years, but had now set up my own PR company and would be ideally placed to assist in his mega new £200 million venture.

"Well how are you, Nigel?" came his astonishing reply. "You have clearly forgotten, but you were always so helpful to me back in the days when I organised the Nailsea Carnival!"

Ian invited me over to his office where I learned that JT Baylis, was proposing to develop this giant out of town shopping complex, only a stone's throw from the M5, in partnership with, the Prudential Corporation, and that he would recommend that, Media-Consult, should represent them.

This his client agreed to do and within a few weeks, I was boarding a London train at Yatton to go to meet the corporation's head of marketing, who agreed that it made perfect sense to have one PR man representing both parties.

From then on, I was a regular visitor to Ian's office and I remember him laying out huge drawings showing the extra feeder lanes that were going to be needed to funnel tens of thousands of shoppers' cars on and off the M5 at its already busy junction with the A38.

It was also fascinating paying update visits to this huge building site, with its anchor John Lewis and Debenhams stores at either, end and watching it literally growing out of the ground around me.

Once the scheme was well advanced, with palm trees in massive planters being craned into position along the main retail hall, and dozens of shop units on both levels, the Prudential Corporation's marketing people, decided to hold a big marketing event in a large marquee.

I was charged with arranging for a helicopter to take members of the media up for a birds-eye view of the complex.

Luckily for me, my Cosmic Joker did not intervene on this occasion!

It was also suggested that my team and I might like to prepare a list of suitable names for the complex and this proved to be a real challenge because nothing seemed to quite fit the brief, even though we wracked our brains for those names with an historical or geographical context.

I don't believe the marketing people at the Pru faired any better than we did because, in the end, and perhaps by default, it was decided to call the complex, Cribbs Causeway, which after all was the name of the area.

OFFICE LIFE

I think I can honestly say that in the 17 years I operated Media-Consult from, The Garage House, in Wrington, with the help of former colleagues and friends, Paul Fluck, Dave Baxter, Peter Gibbs, and later, Pat Randall, editor of the former Bristol Observer, and of course not forgetting, Kerry Bee, that there was ever a cross word spoken.

But there was quite understandable outrage, when I came into the office one morning with a pint of skimmed milk for our coffee and Peter, an accomplished poet. was promptly moved to pen the following ode, **You've Got Us Under Your Skim**:

> We cows do have a hard, hard life
> We're out in wind and rain
> And herded daily out to grass
> Then back to shed again.
> We're driven over nasty roads
> Through horrid slush and mud
> And hardly have the chance between
> To quietly chew the cud.
> Our udders once knew maidens' hands
> Not soul-less rubber pumps
> No wonder we are moo-ved to tears
> And often in the dumps.
> But still our milk is of the best
> The cream as you might say
> The White Stuff is the nation's drink
> And long we pray may stay.
> Yet there are those so unimpressed
> They snub us at their whim
> And choose to pour into their cup
> The stuff that's known as skim.
> The goodness has been drained away
> Just leaving thin white water
> We might as well give up right now
> And trundle off to slaughter.

At 1pm Peter, Dave and I, and later accompanied by Pat, would stroll across the road to The Plough Inn for a drink and a tapas lunch.

Peter, Pat, and I, would always play a game of Rummy, which Peter invariably won – Dave meanwhile playing the one-armed bandit - and then we would return promptly at 2pm.

Now Peter would go straight to his computer and look for the play on words, based. on food and the name of a city, town, or village, which Dave would have pinged over to his computer screen before lunch, and immediately try to better it; for example. Bakewell, Eggseter or Birming-ham.

Believe it or not, this little game went on for several years before they finally ran out of ideas.

I got into trouble again one Christmas, when I accidentally picked up a packet of vegan mince pies from the little village shop opposite, to have with our morning coffee, and again there was some quite understandable outrange, as usual, sparked off by Peter, who said that the cardboard packet had more flavour than the contents.

I always hosted our annual Christmas office party, with wives and partners, at the former Pizza Provencale in Clifton, just down the road from Bristol's famous Suspension Bridge, but there was one other small office tradition which was always observed.

We did not have a Christmas tree, but used the individual silver foil trays from those morning coffee mince pies, to create mini-Christmas decorations, which were then lined up along a shelf, with a small prize being awarded to the one considered the most artistic.

Christmas was the season when I invariably became the target for jokes concerning my appalling handwriting, which I had to admit was bad then, but is even worse now, and inevitably led to Peter penning a poem.

PITY THE POOR POSTIES!

Oh pity the poor Posties
Who work near Nigel's friends
For every year at Christmas
To them his cards he sends.

He writes just like a spider
That's had too much to drink
And then been forced to line dance
With legs all dipped in ink.

It's not so bad for sorters
They've got high-tech machines
For working out them hieroglyphs
Once read by ancient queens.

Their scanners can do Sanskrit
Chinese, Russian and Greek
Yet out there on the pavements
It's Nige of whom they speak.

Their sacks should carry tidings
Of festive peace and cheer
But all you hear are curses
As at his scrawl they peer.

Envelopes at arm's length
Held up to the light
"It must be here," they mutter
"If sorters got it right."

They knock at likely houses
Cry out if folk they spy
"D'you know a chap called Nigel?
"His friend must live nearby."

> They call at local pharmacies
> Who well know doctors' script
> To work out just one letter
> Would really be a gift.
>
> Then through some Yuletide magic
> They finally reach their goal
> Pop the card through letterbox
> And back to base they stroll.
>
> As round their tree they settle
> There comes a mighty shout
> "You're very nice young Nigel –
> "But please just TYPE IT OUT!!"

Most sunny afternoons, I would step away from my desk for a short stroll around the village, including the occasional contemplative sit on a shady seat in the centuries-old parish churchyard.

I encouraged everyone else to do the same and said to Kerry on several occasions that if she wanted to go out between jobs and pick up some shopping, I would not mind in the slightest, but surprisingly, no one ever did follow my example.

One of my prime motivators for flying off on feature-writing trips for Lloyds List, back in my Port of Bristol days, was that it helped to satisfy my life long thirst for travel.

So once Media-Consult was firmly established with a steady income from a range of clients, and always at least two colleagues, on whom I could depend, in the office, I simply could not resist the temptation of taking off for a week's organised group trekking all around Europe and the Mediterranean, at least six times a year!

Peter and I would also take off on occasion, and besides walking the famous Offa's Dyke, we went on our two railway journeys across America.

These mini adventures are featured in, Paths and Poetry, our Amazon published book, which celebrates more than 40 years of walking across Britain together, with me writing travel features for syndication and Peter penning poems along the way.

It was Dave, who would normally drive over to nearby Yatton Station and pick me up after my latest jaunt and update me on all the happenings during my absence.

Then it was back to the usual round of calling or visiting clients and writing press releases.

In business mode, I had always listened to my inner voices, and made a point of acting on them immediately.

'Why don't you give so and so a call because you haven't spoken to him or her for ages?' was the question that would pop into my head now and again and, on those occasions, I would act on that prompt immediately.

Not for the first time the response would be: "That is funny because I was only thinking of you the other day," but every once in a while, I would make that call with a spectacular result.

A fine example of this was the sunny afternoon I was strolling along the beach in Budleigh Salterton with my family when that voice popped up and urged me to call one of the members of the old Long Ashton Rural District Council to whom I had not spoken for many years.

It was so long ago that I had to dig out all my old contacts book before finally coming across the ex-directory number and calling it to the great surprise of the recipient.

I explained that I had left the Bristol Evening Post some years earlier and was now running my own PR operation.

"Nigel, how lovely to hear from you and yes I am sure we could use your services," came the reply, with the result that I spent the next three years working with the then, Bristol Development Corporation, one of a number, which the government had set up to kick-start major infrastructure projects.

But the fact that I went on turning a deaf ear to thoughts about closing-down my Wrington operation, was surely a sign of my uncertainty because we all got on so well together.

But after 17 years of continually looking for the next new client, the feeling that perhaps it was time for a change began to quietly grow, a bit like a gentle tapping at a door, until eventually I could ignore it no longer.

I had in the preceding years, been fortunate enough to have an up-side-down oak house, built in the small land-locked orchard behind my Congresbury home with views along the Wrington Vale, and the idea of enjoying a slightly lower key life, finally prevailed.

I think I can say that none of my colleagues wanted our enjoyable professional time together to come to an end and our final stroll over to The Plough for a farewell sit-down lunch was not the most joyous of the occasions.

But no one was leaving empty handed because I passed over the Castle Combe Racing Circuit business to Dave, who could easily continue doing the work from home, but eventually decided to go and live in the apartment. which he and his wife, Pat, already owned in the south of Spain.

Peter took on all the competition and reader offer projects, which had been his baby right from the start, and incorporated them into his existing company, Bellevue Marketing, taking along Hazel Davies, who had been a late addition to the Media-Consult office, joining from the estate agent's office across the road.

Peter lived down the road in Clevedon, but his partner, Sally, lived in Oxfordshire, so the opportunity of spending a lot more time working from her home, now opened up for him.

Kerry, whom I think really preferred going out to work, agreed to go on assisting both Peter and I and did so for many years to come.

I went back to working from home, so after those most enjoyable and fascinating years, the wheel finally turned full circle.

EPILOGUE

After closing the office in Wrington in 2003, I continued working from home in Congresbury until meeting my second wife and keen gardener, Jenny, and moving to her cottage on a hillside in Monmouthshire.

Believe it or not, Peter and I are still working part time. While I retain three long-standing PR clients, whom I now regard more as friends, Peter is still running his luxury hotel marketing enterprise.

Having walked together for over 40 years, with me writing features about our adventures, and Peter penning poems along the way, we decided to publish a book on Amazon, called Paths and Poetry.

Peter looked after the editing as he had done for a number of books, including his two poetry anthologies, Let The Good Rhymes Roll, my five-part family saga, Albany House, and my book of travel features, Going Abroad.

The little life-long voice in my head then piped up: "'Now I'll tell you what's missing and that's your career in journalism!'

Needless to say, it could not be ignored and Peter once again took on the editing of this story of my highly eventful life in regional newspapers and public relations, during a career spanning more than 40 years.

As you will have read, it was my initial training and later my real passion for my role as the then Bristol Evening Post's Port of Bristol correspondent that went on to open the door to my PR career and all that followed.

I hope I have shone on a light on a pre-internet age when newspapers had a mass readership and provided a vital source of information, long before the advent of social media.

Those were the heady days when reporters would cover the majority of courts, and council meetings, in the latter case providing an essential defence of local democracy.

The lessons learnt on a small town weekly newspaper, were to stand me in good stead in the many fascinating years to follow.

I have, of course, many abiding memories from those earlier times, but there is one that sticks out of the water, like little Denny Island, not far down channel from the Royal Portbury Dock.

It was a Thursday afternoon, not long after, Eric Price, editor of our sister paper, the Western Daily Press, had moved over to edit the Post and I had popped in to the Temple Way office to have my expenses signed.

I must admit to having some feelings of trepidation as I popped my head around his door, because while Eric was a brilliant journalist, he also had something of a fearsome reputation.

Beckoning me to the seat in front of him, he took off his glasses and began polishing them furiously.

"You" he said without looking up, "have been a thorn in my side for years!"

STOP PRESS

Nigel, centre, and Peter, right, with (from the left) Bob, Bowen, Frances Hardcastle, plus Bronte, and Kerry Bee. Picture: Claire Bowen.

My former colleagues assembled for a reunion lunch at The Plough Inn, Wrington, in July, 2023, and later posed for this picture outside the old Media-Consult offices.